Man...

An eclectic ... management tips.

Phil Larson gets called by the aliases of Dr. Dad, Dr. Phil, Guru, Teach, Boss, Hermano Filipe, and Mr. In-Plant, even though I never invented any of those. My most precious titles are husband, dad, and friend. After all, management starts in our personal relationships. It is for life that we work.

30+ years of managing and still doing it.

Power Principle Choices: These subjects were selected by members of teams I've managed as their favorite sayings learned working with me. In a surprise session, they unveiled a 31 day flip book with key sayings they heard over and over. Apparently, they are such a part of my vernacular they decided to keep notes. **Managers are teachers.**

After working with a team in one company, I met for lunch with the manager. It had been ten years since I worked in the company or with the team. He had been on that team.

He shyly said, "We still use the PAL method."

I responded, "What is the PAL method?"

He then explained that I had signed every directive and procedure with my initials, PAL. They had studied the methods behind the memos and made a system out of them. That is an honor. But, I reminded him they should be learning and growing and not get too bound in prior principles. However, **principles are timeless**. Look for the principles.

If it works for them, then I am honored. If it works for them it will work for you. There are a few others I snuck in besides the 31 and some I left out for the next book.

Enjoy a Better Life Forward. ;-{) phil

Management is a craft. A craft is when talent is developed with training and application. There needs to be a base talent for leading and managing on which you build. Expand knowledge and skill and mix a little artistic individual expression. No two individuals manage exactly the same. How boring would that be?

After years of studying, going to classes, getting degrees, learning from mentors, reading every day, teaching in conferences, counseling with mentees, and just plain doing the do, one of my frustrations is the secretive nature of leaders. It seems they want you to drag the most important tips out of them. Really, that is intentional. A good leader never gives away everything. In fact, I'm going to give away the unspoken rule of leadership that did not make it into the team member selection, because I rarely state it publicly.

"Hold wisdom close. Only release it to anticipating learners."

One wise wisdom steward said it this way. "Correct a fool (someone who does not want your correction) and he will turn and shame you with it." Ouch! How true. Over time, when a leader meets this truth a few times, she becomes guarded with what she shares and with whom.

Copyright 2015, Philip A. Larson

Cover photo compliments of Robb Harper.
http://www.robbharper.com

Phil Larson, Director of The Community Transformation Initiative

Manage Well- email considerwell@gmail.com

Index of Ideas: Contents

"A deep south highway patrolman motioned over the man and his truck. They had been travelling 30 mph over the speed limit and trash in the truck bed had been spewing up and down the highway. The patrolman was a little frustrated when he asked the man, "Do you have any ID?"

"Idee 'bout what?" came the reply.

All of us have ideas. Some work and some don't. These ideas are ones that have stood the test of time, multiple teams, multiple industries, 24 hour businesses, and were selected by those using them.

Here are a few of my "idees". If one seems odd, just let it fly down the road like the trash out of the back of the truck. But, trust me, some of them are going to crash into your windshield and you need to stop and assess your direction.

You can just start reading the book and then you don't need an index. No idea here will take you more than a few minutes to read or less than a lifetime to absorb.

The following index takes the ideas and organizes them into Self Development, Principles of Leadership, and Team Development.

I do not ascribe to the thought that a person is a leader or a manager. A leader must manage. A manager must lead. Be both. Your family, community, and workplace need you to be both in all places.

There are a couple of blank pages in the back for notes. Also, there is sufficient space along the way to write in the margins. Read with a pen or pencil in hand. My greatest compliment is to find a marked up book.

Enjoy a Better Life Forward. ;-{) phil

Table of Contents

Leader / Manager Self Development

The Three Hats of a Mature Manager: Syncing Yourself for the Next Step 7

You Stand for What You Tolerate: Two Intolerable Stances for Any Leader 10

Manage DIRFT: Quit Putting out Fires! 4 Attention Items. 13

Face and Voice: Essential Communicators 16

Pareto for Managers Building People.. 19

There is No Box: You are not who you are. It just looks that way.. 35

The Fearful and the Brave 89

Principles of Leadership / Management

The Five P's of a Manager's Portfolio Allow Right Building............ 22

Document – Publish – Train – Measure DPTM................................ 24

Busting Barriers: Two Tips To Activate Leadership in Others......... 28

Lead with Solutions: Five Key Phrases to Lead 32

A Letter to a Young Friend and Budding Entrepreneur 38

Reasonable Price and Trusted Service... 67

The 3 Questions 69

Renaissance Man – There is No Box 72

Razor Sharp Relationships – 10 Risk Taker Tips............................... 74

Change is Never Straight 46

Are you a PMO or a PCO?.. 49

Team Building - Other Development

Kill the Vine: No More Gossip.. 40

The Rule of Synergy: Three Have to Have Accelerators 43

Exceptions Are Not Rules: 3 Safe Guards 53

Fix the Plumbing 56

Presence Communicates Production Priority............................... 59

The Road to Human Loyalty- A Forever Journey 61

Vacation Reverses Progress: Reinforce Routines on Return 64

4 As of Team: Identify Structure 77

4 As of Team: Accountability and Adherence............................... 80

4 As of Team: Action and Alliance 83

Training Tenacity 86

Solving Workflow with Leadership 91

Build Better Budgets with VISION! 95

Power Living For Christians

Christian Power Living Tips!... 97

Risk It! Respect Authority 98

Risk It! Explain Not Excuse 100

Risk It! Find A Way 104

Risk It! Go On Through 107

Risk It! The Better Way Mentality 110

Risk It! Change 114

Risk It! Stand Ground. Give Ground. 117

Risk It! 120

Risk It! Be an Able Also. 123

The Three Hats of a Mature Manager: Syncing Yourself for the Next Step

Don't read this if you are under 35. It won't make much sense. Then again, if you **read and understand it**, you can improve your ability to work well with mature managers and have right development in yourself.

Professionals are intentionally developed. Through involvement in projects and initiatives and departments through your career, the best of who you are is evident. There is a skill to gaining enjoyment and value out of who you are. There is an art to applying that value to your daily business endeavors. **You can be the best you, doing the most fit assignments and have a great amount of fun**. Or not. Choose. Make sure you consider your Three Hats before you choose. Be you.

A friend reminded me that people focus on your weaknesses because they struggle with allowing your strengths. People are like that. They pick at what they don't understand in the most negative ways. But you don't have to let pickiness impact your confidence and connection. You just need to work on your Three Hats.

This above all: to thine own self be true, and it must follow, as the night the day, Thou canst not then be false to any man

William Shakespeare

Three Fields of Play

First, let's take a look at three fields of play. Then we can talk about the Three Hats.

Play to your strength. You know this. Do what you do best. But, you need to really know what that is. Strength can be as limiting as weakness if not tamed. A hard-nosed, goal-driven executive can find herself isolated by dwelling too strong on this strength. Soften the edges of your game. Don't dominate the play, just lead with excellence. People can mistake strength for rigidity. That won't help you or others.

Cover your weakness. Of course you have them. You've found them haunting you every turn of your career. Six courses of style management can't change these core items of who you are. As a manager, I've always had to focus hard on listening. Why? I'm 50+% deaf since birth. So, I arrange my office for optimum face to face contact and limit noise interference. People are usually amazed when I tell them about my limitation as I've mastered masking through sitting in middle spots in conferences and making sure I get directly across from those I expect to be key stakeholders in any meeting. What is yours? Find a cover. Bad note taker? Make sure a good one gets that assignment in every meeting. Take double notes. Find a cover.

Build disciplines. There are some skills that just have to be at a good level whether they are a weakness or not in your specific regimen. Know what they are and find a way to strengthen them. It is not an option to be weak in an area that must be strong. Sorry, it is tough, but you need to fix it. If promptness is hard for you, you must repair. If attentiveness is hard for you, you must repair. You must.

Three Hats: So what the heck am I talking about, Three Hats? Each of us over time discovers from 3-5 core areas of expertise. For me it is operational excellence, communication, and people development. After working multiple companies in multiple industries, these items just keep coming back on top. Sure, I have many skills and abilities like project management and administration and meeting management and facilitating brainstorming, and marketing, and sales, and, and, and… But what are the Three Hats that never come off no matter what I am doing? Find yours. Know them. Develop.

Hat One: This is your core passion. When you get up in the morning, what gets you started? At the end of the day, what are you thinking? What is that core? For me? People development. I love to see people grow.

Hat Two: This is your core performance. Okay, when you example "velocity", where does it happen. Velocity is the ability to do the right thing at the right time that advances you and everyone around you and the business. For me? Operational excellence. Seeing how to adjust an operation to perform the charter is a natural for me and advances the organization.

Hat Three: This is the core producer. This is the trait that makes the other two shine. What is it that you do so well that enables core performance and passion to be energized? This is all about 'vitality'. This puts energy into the performance and keeps you engaged long after others would give up. This secret brings it all together for you. I love encouraging with communication and clarifying with communication and setting vision with communication. Communication enables my passion and let's others walk along and grow the operations.

When your Three Hats are working well they become one hat. The brim, the bill, and the band form one unit for others to see and appreciate. That maturity developed and seen in you can be applied to your next career steps in the position you have or the one you are getting ready to have. Just make sure the hat fits before you engage.

Enjoy a Better Life Forward. ;-{) phil

You Stand for What You Tolerate: Two Intolerable Stances for Any Leader

Tolerance has a clear definition and requires clear standards. When you live with weak tolerance, you live weak. When you live with strong tolerance, others become strong. Any leader must have standards to define the limits of tolerance. Those standards assist in accomplishing vision and mission in both short and long term initiatives.

Who said, "You stand for what you tolerate."? Many would say, "You get what you tolerate". But I like the prior phrase. No way to trace it back to any one person.

The ancient proverbial Solomon wrote, "Out of the fullness of your heart, your mouth speaks." That is pretty close. He wrote more than a few other wisdoms on the need for discipline and vision. You stand for what you tolerate.

There are two intolerable stances for any leader.

Tolerance without standard. How often do we act in fear in our organizations and in front of those we are called to lead by example? Someone points an accusing finger at another's actions and we react in fear of some unknown legality or loss of face in the masses. No leader can lead long without standards. An issue arises and we allow weakness to make decisions because we do not have dedicated enough time to establish our priorities and principles.

A computer installation for a large company hit a standstill. Managers had been pleading for right electrical backup in an area plagued with storms, but *the company standard of "tolerate failure until it costs a fortune or breaks a visible law" was in play.* Now it was getting ready to cost a fortune. Every worker was doing something different and the manager responsible could not direct the mess effectively. Yes, it did cost a fortune to get out of the mess, but standards based risk policy would have deemed the situation intolerable well before the failure and have avoided major expense and exhaustion of staff. You stand for what you tolerate and you get what you tolerate

Standard without tolerance. This one will strangle the best of leadership and organizations. "Well this is the decision of the board and we will implement with no questions." Of course, no decision has thought through every implication or situation that will transpire. Thinking people were dispatched to manage through the muddle. Have you ever made this mistake?

A successful company was hard at work following the directions of the consultant. Why would this group not just comply? These manufacturing based principles must work in service sectors, too, right? Wrong. They would work with some revision, but not straight out of the guru box. Smart managers needed to be allowed to apply the principles in a slightly different manner than the book. The result was a struggle. And with wisdom, in this instance, *the team managers prevailed and were allowed to make right modifications.* The result was a 40% decrease in costs alongside a service turnaround deliverable that went from 10 days to 2 days on a regular basis. A strict adherence to the standard would have brought everything to a standstill and crushed the teams involved. Team members were energized and worked for years coming up with improvement after improvement because tolerance was built into the standard.

Summary: You stand for what you tolerate. You get what you tolerate. These two intolerable stances can cost you major progress and undermine morale and loyalty. They are quite common. Take a few minutes this week to mull over your standards and ensure you haven't violated these. If you have, you are suffering now. The evidence may not have surfaced. It will. And it will cost you in ways you would not tolerate if you realized it.

> *A standard is a measurement tool. Everyone measures up differently to the standard. Tolerance maintains a standard and allows for growth.*

Manage DIRFT: Quit Putting out Fires! 4 Attention Items.

Overwhelming issues seem to have some similar roots. A disaster or two can send any organization or business into a spin. Resource management is challenged. How often does the inattention to right details at right moments create the spin? How often is the spin self-initiated?

Operations can be smooth. They must be effective. DIRFT needs managed.

DIRFT? Do It Right The First Time. This simple acronym should entertain the attention of every executive and manager. Engage it. Paint it on your forehead. Demand it. Coach it. Live it.

Control what is knowable: U.S. Grant was an amazing manager of DIRFT. It turned the war his direction many times. On one occasion General Sherman wrote this about him. "The campaign of Vicksburg, in its conception and execution, belonged exclusively to General Grant, not only in the great whole, but in the thousands of its details…. No commanding general of any army ever gave more of his personal attention to details."

Grant did not leave anything to chance. Faced with a myriad of unknown items, he mastered doing each item under his control as a known. By ensuring all that was under his control was handled correctly the first time, he reserved the strength of his troops for the unknown. The mental acuity necessary to adjust is freed when the known details are handled right the first time.

Plan for the unknowable: Our state and city has a group named VOAID, Volunteer Organizations Assisting in Disaster. During recent repetitive storms, this concert of concern was a first phone call. Coordination made response quick and right. Before federal resources had a chance to open the mail, these teams had already solved a myriad of needs. Having worked together in other disaster situations, these folks made a difference. Others have risen and joined ranks with them and the next disaster will be handled even more smoothly. Do it right the first time.

Quiet Time Development: Building **solutions that work** the first time takes quiet time. Avoid this and DIRFT turns into DRIFT. The operation will drift to the loudest complaint and worst problems. The business will lose vitality and focused expression. Niche will become nice. Nice operations could easily become eliminated operation as they miss the mark on needed activities and only tend to please people on the surface not the deep points of need.

Sharp managers and executives use quiet times to sort the nice from the needed and the issues from the answers. Make sure your plans **fulfill the objectives** of the operation established with reflective thought and right information to enable right decisions.

DIRFT! Do it right the first time. **Inspect what you expect. Expect what you inspect.** When a plan of operation is launched, it needs measurement points established to steer actions. Quality control is fine if you are looking to lose. Make plans that steer quality at each decision point instead of waiting until a job is complete to discover it is bad. Rework is painful. Plan DIRFT purposefully. Teach it. Coach it. Motivate to excellence to prevent constant rework. Learn some simple LEAN principles and implement them to take out wasted time and efforts so operations focus on getting it done right not finding out when it is done wrong.

Summary: There is always enough time to do it right the first time. There is never enough time to keep doing it over and over and over. But, you need an operational plan to do it right. Just giving it to people and expecting them to figure it out is a sure route to failure and frustration. Engage them in the solution at the right moments and plan for smooth successful operation.

Enjoy a Better Life Forward. ;-{) phil

> *Have a great day doing what you do. Operations should live in excellence.*

Face and Voice: Essential Communicators

There are certain bridges that are not worth crossing, no matter what others think. Loyalty and relationships are important. Tony Dungy, Quiet Strength

That quote jumps from every picture and presentation I've seen of Tony Dungy. He never needed to say it because his face and voice always say it. You should be like that. Your face and voice define you.

Use your face and voice to communicate needed messages and lessons to those you serve. Engage the power of your passion and allow the deep roots of your heart to be visible. Common management philosophy leads to common results. Great leaders such as Tony Dungy, legendary coach and motivator, allow face and voice to say, "Commitment counts," even when others want to avoid transparency.

Speed of communication does not replace the need for face and voice.

Mass of communication does not replace the value of face and voice.

Repetition of communication does not replace the power of face and voice.

Face and voice communicate beyond words into value, passion, and power.

"Let's discuss this," announces the executive.

A gregarious and generous leader brings comforting value in communications that reaches the heart of those following when face and voice are engaged. An opportunity to discuss with such a person is welcome.

An angry and tempestuous leader stirs anxiety through face and voice. An opportunity to discuss may be avoided.

A pompous and persuasive face and voice bring different understanding to the same words spoken by a serving and heartfelt communicator.

The message can be the same, but face and voice provide platform.

Great leaders are masters of face and voice and command control of them at appropriate times and places. Greatness of communications comes out of the transparency of that face and voice. Sure there are false faces and feigned voices of politician leaders. You don't have to be in politics to lead politically. You don't have to be a political leader if you are a politician in the service of the people. Those around the false faced politician discover over time the difference and words become hollow and leadership ability wanes.

One of my great communicator friends is Carey Casey, CEO of the National Center for Fathering. I love to be around Carey and let him rub off on me. During one of our early conversations, upon walking up to me he said, "I remember you, you're the one with the kind face for everyone." His observation shocked me and pleased me. Certainly there are many days my face and voice communicate other stances, but this was the one he received and valued and affirmed. It was a transparent communication back to me of what value I was bringing into relationships. Face and voice communicated for me where letters and email might not. Carey's face and voice will always say to me, "open, honest, forthright, committed" framed in that and other interactions. Every communication I receive from him will be tampered with his face and voice. (Catch Carey at **www.fathers.com**)

Be you. Let that face and voice of your deepest heart come out. Quit hiding behind emails and power point presentations. Take your face and voice out there and engage. Of course there needs to be a compassionate and concerned heart that leads for the good of others for a servant leader, but that is another missive.

Enjoy a Better Life Forward. ;-{) phil

> *Check the heart beneath your face every morning as diligently as you check the exterior face in the mirror.*

Pareto for Managers
Building People

"80% of the results come from 20% of the effort. Focus on the right 20%." Phil

Right this minute, my desk is a mess. Multiple projects for clients and engagements in the non-profit sector press for attention. How do I decide what to pick up and what to put down? Building the people around me seems the best and most prudent decision to engage effectiveness. Those built today become power for tomorrow.

The decision mechanism of important versus urgent seems inadequate. Important plus urgent must be priority one. Important but not urgent brings best results and is priority two. Not important but urgent earns a three. Finally, not important and not urgent should go to a trash bin or some holding pattern for when it changes to something that needs attention.

Executives and managers can make multiple critical decisions every hour. Sometimes it seems there are multiple decisions each minute. There is a way to sort. There is a way to prioritize and get optimum results.

Rebellion to tyranny is obedience to God. Thomas Jefferson

Maybe this quote is a little out of place for the discussion. Or is it? Is the tyranny of urgent matters as tyrannical as a king in a country across the ocean? Maybe it is closer to home and more impactful on bad and disorderly living than a governmental system could be. Somehow, I don't think Jefferson was pointing us to Godliness as much as making a strong position for self-governance. Self-governance reduces tyranny of the urgent

80/20: 80% of results come from 20% of the people. 80% of sales come from 20% of the customers. 80% of our smiles come from 20% of our thoughts. On and on we can make comparisons of 80% from 20% whether they are true or not. This is not a rule but a guideline. In the work of developing people it is most applicable when you focus on the right 20%.

The Right 20% Takes Right Approach

Stimulate Creative Thought: This is a right 20% in developing others. Don't just allow creative thought, stimulate creative thought. Management by the book and standard operational procedure can produce quality and it can also produce stiff brained obeisance. Robot staff will not produce the right 80%.

Challenge Progress Reports: How often do you open a progress report and wonder if anything of any real value was accomplished? Do you ask questions? Do you get clarification? Are you managing for effective, right results or just results? Our desire to please others and do the expected job can cause us to use reports as promotional material instead of decision making material. Unchallenged over time, everyone can get caught in meaningless redundancy and semantic fluff.

Affirm Specifically: "Good job, Jack." That is a lame statement. "Jack, I appreciate your taking care of the details on this report while providing a succinct executive summary from which I can make a decision." Okay, Jack can curve his future results to match that statement and bring me the 80% effectiveness I need from 20% of his efforts.

Correct in Private: It is tough to resist correction at the time of fault. When coaching a developing team, it was painful to watch failure after failure pile up at an event.

Stupid is as stupid does. Finally, I interjected some correction. The result was an angered staffer, who was doing the best he had been coached in the past. Now, I had to get him aside, heal the pain, and get him reengaged in the success of the moment. Better would have been to take mental notes and review in a post mortem along with all of the successes.

Summary: You can get 80% of results from your staff with 20% of your effort. They can get 80% of their results from 20% of the effort. All the fancy grids and principles are useless if you are not concentrating on the right 80% and the right 20%. Those come from developing your team to target in manners that build the person not just the results. In the end, it is the person that will make the results appear within any system or process or procedure.

Enjoy a Better Life Forward. ;-{) phil

$$\left[\text{Results speak for you in meetings you cannot attend.} \right]$$

The Five P's of a Manager's Portfolio Allow Right Building

Assessing a business operation takes scrutiny of the right five P's. Get it wrong and you can find yourself damaging more than building. Get it right and the right stuff comes together. Look to the heart not the surface. Uncover riches.

Character is like a tree and reputation like a shadow. The shadow is what we think of it; the tree is the real thing. Abraham Lincoln

First Things: Begin with the end in mind. This is another article, but you need to be reminded before you look into the P's. Every operation includes an objective to be measured and met. Don't look too deeply into the organization before you determine this item. Otherwise, the P's, which may be out of position, can lead you to wrong places. If they were perfect, why would anyone need you? They must continually be adjusted to measureable objectives.

People: Take time to review the people set. Are the right passions, personalities, and portions (skills sets) on the team? Is this set to succeed or set to fail? Has this team been intentionally built and honed or sporadically pieced together? What will it take to realign and make productive? What is missing? What is unbalanced?

Props (Tools and Technologies): Examine the tools and technologies in the operation. Are they current? **Are you trying to hit a big hairy audacious goal with skinny, smooth banana peels?** Has the shop been kept upgraded or held back with cost cutting for years? What will be the investment? Is the team "too techy" and loaded up with an oversupply so that no tool is really mastered?

Processes: If you can't document the processes clearly, you don't know what you are doing. Deming said something similar to that. He's right. In one shop, it took two years to get process documentation settled. Development teams kept changing the underlying processes without ever settling on the existing. No one really knew what a good result at the end of the day looked like. After documentation was settled, the team performed smoothly and on time every day according to company needs. This is a touchy and tough area to address. Don't avoid it.

Projects: Projects in motion reveal major needs if they are rightly designed. The lack of defined projects is a sure sign of a disparate, disorderly, and dying operation. Are capital improvements in motion? What services are being designed for future delivery? Is there a training program? Cross training?

Products and Services: Well, why do you exist without these? Service catalogue? Do the focused customer groups know how to get great service and what service is available? What of these are core critical to the overall organization? Why?

Summary: If you take these five P's and write down three notes, you have **the beginning of a great business plan**. 1. What is the inventory or status of the P? Make a list of the items and critical criteria, benefits, advantages, and demographics. Assess alignment to objective and need. 2. What needs changed? 3. What is the impact on the other four P's when I change it?

Business is building. Never stop building.

Enjoy a Better Life Forward. ;-{) phil

Document – Publish – Train – Measure DPTM

Capability maturity models (CMM) for process in management are based on a simple principle. Document what you expect. Publish it to others. Train them. Follow up with measurement to ensure it is being used and results are being achieved as designed. Some years before I knew anything about CMM, this was hammered into me by an astute manager and mentor. This can apply to any area. Don't just focus on daily routines. Think about quarterly reports or employee review handling. What about an organizational change? Is it right to use email and quick information on high impact items while painstakingly covering easy routines? But, we do it, don't we?

You don't have to belong to the training department or use games to get this. **Simple and consistent application** of these principles will win you fans in your team.

Why It Works: When you DPTM, you should consider using as many different modes as possible. Don't just write it down in an email and expect people to understand and follow. It won't happen.

There are seven understood, primary roots of comprehension in learning. People learn differently.

Kinetic – Do it. Touch it. Get physical with it. In a production shop, there are many for whom this is the deepest root of understanding.

Emotional – Yes, some people have to get emotional to 'Get it.' Emotions have a big vocabulary. Anger, hatred, frustration, joy, happiness, anxiety, fear, angst, wild hearted abandon, quizzical, consternation, confusion, engaged, light-hearted, enchanted, apoplexy, fixation, consumed, apathetic, mournful. Some people have to grieve over the last item to receive the next one. Believe it and allow for it. Don't judge team members while they are sorting through emotions. It is a learning process. Now, if they camp on negative emotions, you have some issues to resolve.

Intellectual - Wow. Yes, we all want our team members to study and understand what is happening. But, it is not required for everyone. Yet, for some, a simple instruction will never accomplish mastery. They must engage intellect deeply.

Discussion – Even if the subject itself is not discussed, if there is discussion surrounding the process or procedure, it makes for better understanding. Even a negative discussion can open up the ability to understand. Leave this out at a major risk of disconnecting. I've seen great people leave companies just because this was not handled well.

Music – Ever wonder why that teenager can learn with loud music in the background or why every movie has sound continually? It helps. For some, it is necessary.

Auditory - We all need to hear what is happening.

Visual - Get your eyes on it. Look over the documents. Attach some graphics. This does not mean literal learning. Many visual learners do not connect with the words and paper. They need additional stimulus with color and graphics and maybe even motion.

None of us use only one of these for understanding. Engage them all and you will cover your team's needs. *The more modes of communication, the deeper the message tends to embed.*

What each means: DPTM

Document: When you document a policy or process or procedure, you write it down. That can and should include supporting graphics and video and screen captures where appropriate. Email is not documentation. Email might be a delivery method for a document, but an email itself should never be considered good documentation. Documentation is compliance checked, authorized, categorized, organized, stored, and retrievable. **Back pocket documentation is dangerous.** When each member of the team carries a different version of the process in their "back pocket", you are doomed. Clean out the stashed versions and get down to an authorized view.

Publish: Once you have agreed upon documentation that represents the policy, process, or procedure, you need a communication system that ensures all upstream and downstream team members involved have been notified. Give adequate time for review and questions.

Train: Oh, boy. This one is skipped too often. Well, she should have read it, right? Wrong. Train with the published documentation in hand or on screen. Verify and ask revealing questions that help you understand if they understand. Let the person solo the procedure with the trainer observing. In fact, have the trainer do the process in front of the person before they attempt to solo. Make sure the documentation is readily available for the trainee to refresh. Sometimes you can forget a key point or go long periods between using a procedure and need that original training material alongside at 3am.

Get a sign off. That is not a failsafe. It does challenge the trainee to pay close attention and communicate if it does not make sense to them.

Measure: Include verification and communication of measurement criteria for any routine. This is a good place to make sure the trainee understands what the expected result looks like when the process or procedure is completed or the policy followed. Then implement a measurement tool on a frequency fit to task. Everything doesn't need measured every iteration, but much does and patterns monitored for continuous service improvement.

Enjoy a Better Life Forward. ;-{) phil

> *Manage well. Apply sensible principles. Consider impact. Have fun.*

Busting Barriers: Two Tips To Activate Leadership in Others

Every leader is challenged to develop leadership in key followers. It is frustrating to look out and yearn for true leadership in our team. Yet, we find that people today don't stay with a single company for any length of time. Leadership takes time. You can get long term commitment. It is possible. You have to do things differently.

One of the greatest managers of all history, Solomon, put it this way in his comprehensive book on managing life, relationships, business, and government, **Proverbs**:

To know wisdom and instruction,
To perceive the words of understanding,
To receive the instruction of wisdom,
Justice, judgment, and equity;
To give prudence to the simple,
To the young man knowledge and discretion—

Good Goals: Seems like a good objective. For centuries others have read Solomon's snippets of wisdom. Solomon transmitted what he knew to others that were managing his affairs.

Sun Tzu attempted the same objective from the Chinese war lord perspective and penned, The Art of War. It really is much more about living than dying. It is about managing and relationships in a turbulent society. He was intent in training others.

Others have done the same. My bookshelf is full of snippet books from great managers and leaders. The lessons of great men and women can give us guidance in tough situations.

Time Counts: But, if no one stays the task to work out the wisdom and be developed in the fine nuances, you simply lose your investment. They move on and build another business or organization that may in fact take away from your endeavors. **Astute business managers are not happy when they lose the value of an investment** in either people or property. People are not property. They have wills and emotions and desires and must be treated differently.

Tip One:

Be Loyal: Handle Conflict Up Front and Fast: The common business practice of today is to demand loyalty from staff, yet make decisions without being loyal to them and their families and lives. Making the legal decision is not always a loyal decision. Listening to accusations and gossip concerning staff without direct clarification and consultation is not a position of loyalty but fear and low self-confidence and politicking of the negative kind.

"The first job of a leader—at work or at home—is to inspire trust. It's to bring out the best in people by entrusting them with meaningful stewardships, and to create an environment in which high-trust interaction inspires creativity and possibility." — Stephen M.R. Covey, The SPEED of Trust: The One Thing that Changes Everything

Greatness: A great leader for whom I worked early in my career came into my office with an anonymous letter. It accused me of some indiscretions. They were false. Only with honest and open discussion could we ferret a good response. The letter had gone to the president of the company. We had been in a turnaround organization situation where hard decisions were being made daily. Of course people were not in 100% agreement. Of course people are people. The prior management of the company had been prone to politics and finger pointing. Everyone knew that and knew how to trip the wires to get what they wanted. This new management had better integrity; otherwise, I would not be working for them. By reviewing the letter, we found adjustments we could make that could better the organization results. Backroom politics turned into front office success.

Openers: The leader's opening comment set the stage. "Phil, before you read the letter you need to know that both the CFO and I told the president that this does not sound like you." He started from a position of loyalty and honesty and open communication. We discussed the contents, who might have sent it, why they might have sent it, was there anything I needed to adjust in managing, and moved on. The company came out of a chapter 11 situation in record time and we all enjoyed our time together. Loyalty and trust were the words of the day and the owners received great benefit. I would go to work beside this man again in a minute if the opportunity arose that was mutually beneficial.

Dear Failure, I am writing today.... Failure on this point costs dearly. Typical management style would have been to have secreted the letter into the unofficial personnel file, brooded over the contents, discussed it with others, and promoted politics. That is how most organizations roll. Yes, you do. Admit it and quit it. Little birds leak that style into the hallways and the entire organization suffers loss of key staff at the most inopportune moments. Disloyal behavior in the board room promotes disloyal behavior at the point of customer contact. It is not a secret. Get real and get honest.

Tip Two:

Go Ahead and Share Insights: All of us have insights gained in leadership. Most of us hold them close to the chest and make upcoming leaders dig them out like some buried treasure. Why are you leaving leadership undeveloped by forcing them to guess? Are you afraid you are wrong about what you know is right? Take a few minutes every day to intentionally leak leadership.

An Amazing Gift: Last year my team brought me an amazing gift. It was thirty-one leadership wisdoms they had learned from me over the course of the prior three years. They could repeat them and could apply them. They made them into a flip calendar. I was amazed and humbled. It shocked me that they had discerned so willingly tips of leadership and management and relationship and had integrated them into their work and home habits. Somehow, great leaders had taught me to be open with wisdom and it was building other leaders. Pass it on.

Starting Right: My mind goes back to my first assistant supervisor position. One day I went into the manager's office somewhat nonchalantly for a meeting. He looked me direct in the eye from across his desk. "Phil, go get a pen and paper and come back. Don't ever go into a meeting with a leader without expectation of receiving instruction, noting it, and being responsible to follow up." Now, he probably said something different, but that is what he communicated. Wow! I listened and have repeated that wisdom hundreds of times to those for whom I've had responsibility to develop as leaders. Leak leadership. Do it intentionally.

To Work, Two Work: Do these two and you'll increase your leadership impact. These are core items. They can guide you and prevent major mishaps. Sure, I can tell you stories of when I've violated them or seen others violate them and the destruction it caused. You know those stories. None of us are perfect. But perfect practice might just result in better performance as a leader, longer relationships with other leaders, and some real fun and satisfaction watching development of trusted leadership and sustained organizational progress.

Enjoy a Better Life Forward. ;-{) phil

Lead with Solutions: Five Key Phrases to Lead

There is power in your words, Leader.

Leaders lead. We lead with our words, our actions, our intent, and our example.

Leaders lead. Leading flows from the inner core of a leader outward for followers to follow. Wisdom literature intrigues and builds me. Two principles that regurgitate in my meditative time apply here.

What is in your heart comes out your mouth.

Words carry life or death.

Uncomfortable as that may be for some, it is life and energy for leaders. Those that deny they are being led are fools looking for a place to fail. Those that accept they are both being led and leading others have matured to a grasp of reality needed for contentedness and success. Watching words is a key necessity of leadership.

One of the ways leaders lead is with the entry words they use in conversations and meetings and personal engagements. So let's look at five phrases that lead well and lead to impact and influence.

How can we lead effectively with our entry words?

Lead #1: *How do you feel about this situation?* Leaders fail many times by leading with precooked answers. Try leading with a question. The conversation is headed a positive direction based on your quick and thoughtful lead. Watch out for asking how people think. That will get you 80% less response than asking them how they feel. They will tell you what they think in response to asking them how they feel. For the most part, people are less threatened when asked how they feel than asked how they think.

Lead #2: *There could be some amazing benefit to this approach.* You just opened the other person or group up to a positive view of what follows. Yet, you have not committed anyone to a position of yes or no. The engagement is now open to include a description of the issue being addressed, but with an expectation of a positive outcome. Lead on.

Lead #3: *What worries you most about our issue?* Wow. You just posed an emotional tie to the others in conversation. It is not someone else's issue, but our issue. You've entered into a supportive stakeholder position and communicated you will be there to help work through the blips. At the same time, you gave the other person influence in the next steps.

Lead #4: *Have you considered a possibility of option X?* This is an enticing lead that suggests a solution without forcing compliance. Leadership contains an element of power along with authority. By opening with consideration of an option, meaning there are other options, you give power to the others in the conversation. It can be a big win when working with a strong leader. Some leaders place themselves in defensive stance over a position they have taken in the past. You just graced them with a way out that saves face for them and could bring them better success than a present entrenched option.

Lead #5: *Having considered many options, here is one I'd like to bring to the table for discussion.* Okay, this is a lead based on research prior to this moment. You've opened the discussion to include consideration of other options and problem barbs and even rabbit trails. It is an empowering position for all included. Sometimes an entire room will just go quiet at this point and let you lead forward. Be ready for that. After all, you are a leader.

Summary: Notice none of these leads starts with the issue at hand. All of these communicate co-ownership of the issue and the solution and confidence in a positive outcome. Avoid leading with the issue. My days are full of conversations that start, "Phil, I have a problem." That is a position of weakness. Sometimes the individual just wants to discuss their ideas. Many times they are looking to offload the problem and responsibility. Take responsibility by leading into a solution. Leading with the solution in today's environment can be considered pushy and too strong. Lead with compassion and listening and strength with some key phraseology that reveals intent to engage along with intelligence and ownership. Lead on, Leader.

Enjoy a Better Life Forward. ;-{) phil

> *An unlikely adventure requires an unlikely tool.*
> Mr. Magorium

There is No Box: You are not who you are. It just looks that way.

The first step to change is a **holy dissatisfaction** with the present state.

You are not what you have done or what you are doing. You are what you've become and where **you are going**.

Like that? Makes sense to me. Where are you going? What have you become?

Do you like the answer to both of those questions?   So many times we settle for status quo because of what we have experienced and then work to keep adding to blanked existences and shop patterns and sales attempts that are working to a degree, but never seem to break through to the level of performance we would like.   That is one heck of a long sentence. Mull on it for a minute.

We settle for status quo.

We get comfortable with prior experience.

We labor at the common and comfortable.

Eventually it is dull and boring and feels like a blank.

Our workplace becomes **patterned for problems**.

We like the problems with which we are familiar. We know how to fix them.

Our sales are structured and predictable.

The circle remains unbroken.

Deep inside, we yearn for a new level of productivity.

We want to grow.

We want to become more than we have become.

We want to go where we have never gone.

Familiar?

Remember T. S. Seisel? Of course you do. He is American and world history. As a young man his political cartoons graced many key magazines. His 15 years of ad work for Standard Oil helped build the company. Working with Frank Capra, he produced animated training films for soldiers of WWII. Still don't remember him? That was the majority of his life.

Oh, the middle most S? Seuss. Dr. Seuss.

The first book was rejected 27 times. At the time he was a famous cartoonist. Rejected. What had become of him?

Then the Cat in the Hat project just seemed to expose a different man than any had ever met. Over the years, he had become and was becoming someone much different. Where he was going was an unknown until that book well into his career.

Every one of us has that potential in every part of what we do. So many organizations settle for mediocrity. The incredible potential bottled in their staff just sits and stews all the way to retirement. It gets so bad, companies begin giving away the mature workers because the organization has doomed them to zombies through saying, "No", to creative becoming idea after powerful results changing idea. The source of great ingenuity and innovation that resides in the years of wisdom and experience is put aside for youthful energy who have yet to become much of anything. They will. Given time, we all do. Most likely they will become zombies like their predecessors.

Seisel broke mode. It was a persistent and purposeful pursuit inside of him that broke mold. He just refused to quit growing and becoming.

You have systems of work, opportunities for new product, and development of people ahead of you. **What can you become? Where can you go? Oh, the thinks you can think.**

Enjoy a Better Life Forward. ;-{) phil

> *Holy dissatisfaction breeds disruptive discontent and may unearth a solution overlooked.*

A Letter to a Young Friend and Budding Entrepreneur

This letter went to a young entrepreneurial friend of mine sometime back. He was struggling with a decision to try or not. There are some key points for anyone working on a change or transition.

The life of a small business operator (change agent) is tough. You will make less per hour than if you worked at McDonald's flipping burgers for the first few years. You will work for nothing but the love of work and the passion of your idea. If you cannot do that, quit and go to work for someone else. Over time, you can make millions of dollars. In the beginning you will live on beans and peanut butter and tuna fish and learn to like it. You will live in the junkiest apartments and drive old cars. You will put your money into your business and into giving to others. Later, you will have some money. Don't count on it for the first five years. *Everything should go back into the business in some form*.

A small business operator (change agent) can make no excuses. There is no one to blame for any failure or lack of money but you. The economy is not to blame. The customer is not to blame. Ignorance is not to blame. Only you are to blame. Get over blaming others and circumstances. Get ready to face the mirror every morning and *hold yourself accountable* to your vision and your dream and your actions or lack of actions.

Opportunities multiply as they are seized. Sun Tzu. That is pure truth. Every time an opportunity is in front of you, you must answer yes or no quickly. Every one you let pass is gone. Quit whining about the fish you did not catch and go fishing for the next one. There is not time to whine about what did not work. Get over it and get moving forward.

Small business operators fail for lack of planning and lack of execution. That is about the whole of it. The longer you think about what you are going to do, the less you will succeed. **Study, think, plan, and then do**. Be decisive in your ways. **Take knowledgeable action**. It is better to fail while you are acting than to fail while you are sitting and thinking.

You will fail over and over and over. That is just the way life works. **Failure is your teacher**. Failure because you did not plan and did not work the plan is simply stupidity. There is no excuse for stupidity. God did not make you stupid. Sitting around and whining and blaming people and circumstances makes you stupid.

Every day you must study your profession and what affects success. Every day. You are a student forever from this point forward. Read magazines, trade journals, newsletters, and books. Read, read, and read. Blow up the television and the games and social media sites and read.

Go to school. Get as many meaningful certifications and degrees as possible in the next five years.

Sleep is a waste of time. Sleep the exact amount needed to stay healthy and alert.

So, if this is what drives you and makes your clock tick, **DO IT!** Quit thinking and whining. DO IT!

Enjoy a Better Life Forward. ;-{) phil

Kill the Vine: No More Gossip

"I don't take requests for people who are not in front of me. That's called gossip."

Every manager must intersect with this issue. Every manager must stop this issue as soon as it comes. You cannot let gossip abide in your team. No greater destructive force exists in the workplace.

What is gossip? Gossip is a negative leaning comment spoken by one person about another person who is not in the present conversation. Sorry if you don't agree, that is my definition and I stick to it. After leading tens of thousands of constituents, members, and workers, this definition helps limit pain and promote a healthy environment.

What does it sound like? "Well, have you heard Jay is having trouble at home?" Innocuous? Hardly. This is a loaded, pain giving, detrimental, and judgmental statement that has no place in a healthy work environment. Managers, you need to get this out of your meetings. You need to get this out of your hallways and back rooms. This is political minded manipulation and leads to the wrong decisions and conclusions.

Where does it come from? Sometimes it has a compassionate root. We really want to be tender and understanding toward others. How many times have I said something like this? Too often. That is why managers must have a no nonsense approach to prohibiting. All of us slip into these thoughts. Humans just do it. Our nature leans to wanting to include others in our judgments for affirmation of ideas. But, it hurts others.

Where else does it come from? Sometimes it is simply poisonous. Yes, there are many who live to manipulate the thinking of those around them. Of course you know who they are. They are attached to the rumor vine in the work place and incipiently receive and feed the monster. Ever had a good associate maligned by the vine and lose credibility? It happens. The most astute executives fall prey to listening to viners and forgetting the source of the slander. We allow hall talkers to get into our circle and affect our decision making.

How do you stop it? You can't. But you can limit influence on yourself and you can constrain the amount flowing in your teams. *One third shift worker came to me in a shop and complained about having to hear continual negative talk from other workers. Night shifts get boring. People don't have access to all the day information. Gossip flows. It was a good time for some intervention. One by one I met with each night, second, and day shift worker on the team. One by one, I looked each of them in the eye. One by one, I gave each of them permission to respond to any company or non-company person and say the following statement when another would start a negative complaint about another team member. "That person is my co-worker. I like to think well of them. I'd prefer you did not make negative comments to me. Why don't you talk directly to them?"* When a predatory maligner hits that wall a few times, they tend to take the pain to some other group in their life like church or family or the bar down the street. Gossip loves the path of least resistance.

What if there is truth to it? So? Truth is not the issue. Negative conversation is the issue. When my children begin to learn some reason (three years old), I instruct each of them this way. "Don't tattle on your brother. If he is doing something dangerous, come tell me. Otherwise, just talk to him." **Hopefully, your team is older than three**. Of course if a team member is doing drugs on the job or being malicious or not following procedures action needs taken. Team members may have not been able to reach them or feel threatened if they try. Then, it must be moved up the chain. Maybe a couple of coworkers can get together with the person (not alone behind the back) and talk it out before running it up the manager pole.

What happens if you don't address it? It will eventually undermine the performance of the team. Negative politics is a painful way to live and inefficient in decision outcomes. The cumulative effect will strip away at morale. People will avoid creative thought and innovation. A dull zombie glaze might be noticed in the team when it reaches advanced stages.

Summary: My hard line stance of not taking requests for another person communicates quite clearly. When a coworker of Jack comes with the seemingly harmless, "Jack would like to take next Friday off." I respond with, "I'd be glad to entertain Jack's request. Why not have Jack ask me, himself?" and go on with good managing. Communicate open concern along with privacy.

At the lake, I have an acre in the woods. Poison ivy likes to vine and pop up in the shade of the trees. Every spring, out comes the herbicide and I walk the property and kill every leaf I can find of the stuff. When I started doing this it took an hour and even some digging up of vines. After three years, it takes a few minutes. if you stop a vine when the sprout pokes through the ground, you don't have to deal with a thumb thick vine or an hundred instances at the base of every tree.

Enjoy a Better Life Forward. ;-{) phil

The Rule of Synergy: Three Have to Have Accelerators

"The whole is greater than the sum of the parts." Phil

Engage others in creative and synergistic endeavors. Purposefully find ways to force team member interplay for power results. Be sensitive and firm. This is not a day at the ropes course. This is in the work place on real tasks that have real risk of failure and real potential for success and reward.

"Ineffective people live day after day with unused potential. They experience synergy only in small, peripheral ways in their lives. But creative experiences can be produced regularly, consistently, almost daily in people's lives. It requires enormous personal security and openness and a spirit of adventure." Steven Covey

It takes a LEADER: Good executive leaders understand this rule. Leadership is required. Manager thought tends to avoid this risky behavior. Lead.

Personal Security: The workplace should ooze with personal security and powerful self-esteem and a sense of individual dignity. Of course it might not be happening where you lead. Then you need to work on it. People need to understand accountability and responsibility and the safety of making mistakes from which we learn.

Accountability means I understand my actions and results impact all those around me and I account that into my decisions. Others will hold me accountable for what I do. They will rejoice in tandem, forgive forthright mistakes, and hold me responsible for results both individual and together.

Responsibility means my action will impact me directly. I get it. I understand it. I welcome it. Good or bad results, I am responsible for my actions.

Personal security can only be reinforced in such a dual environment. Many lack personal security and are looking for everyone from mom and dad to the government to supervisors to take responsibility for their success or failures. Those people cannot thrive in synergy at optimum levels. But they can start where they are, grow, and experience more daily.

Openness: Every team has to find the place of what Jim Collins calls, "brutally confronting the facts." It is not negative. It is a direct and non-personal approach to dealing with the blips, glitches, misstatements, wrong turns, customer complaints, and missed deadlines. Dancing around the issues because a team member is overly sensitive inhibits synergy. You have to want synergy. You have to desire synergy. You have to yearn for synergy to get past covered conversations into open, intelligent discussion.

Spirit of Adventure: A community leader speaking at a business leaders' lunch asked for a show of hands. "Who loves to do things with uncertain results and a high risk?" Only one hand among 450 went up. "Well", he said, "that is the definition of adventure." Among all of these senior executives, bankers, lawyers, CEOs, and wizened warriors of the workplace, the sense of adventure had died. For synergy to happen every day, the third ingredient is a spirit of adventure. Individually and together the team needs to lead into a continual spirit of adventure.

On a powerfully synergistic team, a client came with a bothersome technical improbability. Theoretically, what they were doing should work. But, it was failing at several levels of production and the supporting vendors had sent them to us for resolution. After some frustrating attempts, one of the team just would not let it go. He tested and tried and worked with the other members to come up with a solution. At first, we discovered how to force it through our production engine, but only with effort. Then synergy exploded. A simple solution was implemented that allowed the originating production shop to perform without having to upgrade their equipment or outsource the job to us. Our team invented themselves synergistically out of a job that was highly profitable. Openness means honesty. Sense of personal security means do the right thing for the client. Spirit of adventure means taking on the improbable and finding a way to do it anyway.

Enjoy a Better Life Forward. ;-{) phil

> Many people have not really experienced even a moderate degree of synergy in their family life or in other interactions.
> They've been trained and scripted into defensive and protective communications or into believing that life and other people can't be trusted.
> This represents one of the great tragedies and wastes in life, because so much potential remains untapped - completely undeveloped and unused, Ineffective people live day after day with unused potential.
> They experience synergy only in small, peripheral ways in their lives.
> Stephen Covey

Change is Never Straight

Controlled chaos is a normative term in the management of change. Change is never straight. Change defies a linear constraint. Change is messy and change is curved. **Leaders must be curved people.**

Mentoring a growth team, we reviewed normal impact of change on the growth leader. In this model vision leads to planning and implementation leads to problems and pressures leads to perseverance leads to accomplishment and success leads to celebration and rejoicing leads to increased vision. Or you can choose crisis instead of perseverance which leads to exhaustion and withdrawal can lead to restoration can lead to increased vision. Or crisis can abort the progress. There are hundreds of divergent paths that may happen. Change is messy and curves a lot.

Change is not for straight line people. They are good at regular performance and processes. Change bothers them. A leader must learn to be a curved person. Change is inevitable and needed. Leaders lead through the curves.

There is one major curve in change you should explore and master. It is the curve between your starting level of productivity and your landing level of productivity. In that curve lies all the potential for disaster and triumph. In that curve many leaders lose sight of vision. In that curve success is assured and failure is certain. Master the curve and master change.

Starting Level: Preceding productivity curve is your present level of productivity and accomplishment. How successful are you? What are your measurements? Know them and get them recorded.

CHANGE CURVE

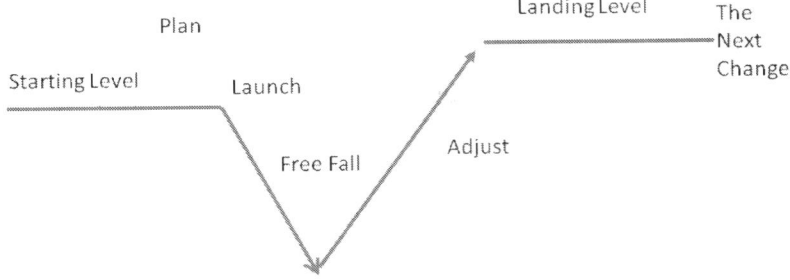

Plan: Now, plan the change that you intend to take your business or other endeavor into the next level of productivity. Go from 100 widgets a day to 200 widgets a day. Add a new product line while keeping current production levels on others. Penetrate a new market. Implement improvement in service. Change for growth.

Launch: Launch the change. Communicate, take action, and plunge into the change. Paralysis by analysis is deadly. There is a moment and point of demarcation. Take it. Fall off the mountain. That's right fall off the mountain of your current productivity level.

Freefall: Change causes freefall. Problems come from change. Teams get confused. Productivity decreases while people absorb new information. The right screw becomes the wrong screw. Questions abound. Production plummets. This was in your plan, right? You made allowance for this, correct? No? Whoops. Fingers get pointed. Doubt crawls up the ladder to challenge the change rationale.

Adjust: Light shines. People push through learning curves. The services straighten out on the planned track. There is smiling in the camp instead of groaning. You knew you would get here, you just wished it had happened on schedule and without the problems. The changes begin to push productivity above your starting level.

Landing Level: Why endure the pain of change? Reach new levels. Plan diligently. Execute well. Adapt strong. Obtain outcomes. Receive reward. Of course, it does not always look so pretty. You might drag onto the landing level scarred and scattered.

Summary: This conversation is one I've had with hundreds of learning leaders. Every new leader expects smooth change, gets into the curve, panics, and needs some encouragement. Have your eyes open when you enter the change curve. You still might get blindsided, but you will be ready. Adapt with good and frequent communication and intentional feedback points. Go ahead and fall off the mountain. The landing spot is higher than where you stand.

Enjoy a Better Life Forward. ;-{) phil

> *Change is inevitable.*
> *Accept that version of reality and it*
> *will be easier to digest.*

Are you a PMO or a PCO?

Entitlement breeds discontent. There really is no productive way to look at entitlement. Don't read this if you like entitlement organizations. Don't read this if you enjoy getting something for existing in your chair.

"The problem with socialism is that you eventually run out of other people's money." Margaret Thatcher

Business, NGO, and government must face the question. Are you a PMO or a PCO?

"You have to do your own growing no matter how tall your grandfather was." Abraham Lincoln

PMO - Poverty Maintenance Organization

PCO - Positive Change Organization

PMOs proliferate under social thrusts. The easy part of being a charitable organization is asking people to give for compassionate repair and reparation and life needs. Food, clothes, housing, and basics are all needed. People will give to maintain a certain level of poverty in another's life. Poverty is the mentality that there is never enough resource and my efforts will never be rewarded adequately. Poverty is a codependent focus instead of an interdependent cooperation. Poverty is not an economic condition. Lack of economic resource is a result of poverty mentality and living. **Societies and organizations that promote systemic adaptation to low rewards encourage economic, moral, and mental poverty.**

PMOs proliferate under corporate mentality. Oops, you thought this was about charities. Any business that pursues entitlement mentality of 'get the minimum done to get paid and get benefits' is as life force destructive as a charity giving out groceries to people who need growth. Businesses that emphasize fun and frivolity and fairness and equality usually end up with a work force bent on work avoidance and entitlement expectation. Those are all good things. They need to be built alongside productivity and profitability. After all business is about a fair return on investment. Jobs happen when profits happen.

PMO is the way of life of the government.
Government consumes more and more of the community resource as laws get added and modified and bureaucracy grows and grows. *It is impossible for all the government entities to pay off the exorbitant early retirement programs that are inequitable and inconsistent with business productivity. More and more cities, states, and nations have reached bankrupt points of no return.* PMO.

How do you become a PCO when you are a PMO?

Positive change organizations proliferate under **reward and recognition**. Now, reward and recognition do not mean everyone gets the same dole or the longest tail gets the biggest piece of the pie. In a PCO, reward comes in relation to **present contribution** not position or power or political expertise.

Productive Behavior and Growth

Shock and Fear

Productive Reward Arrangement Based on Consequence

Communication of Change

State of Entitlement

In parenting theory we call that love and logic. Raising children in a positive environment keys on establishing positive and negative consequences for behavior. Reinforce that environment consistently and a productive citizen is formed. Oh, that is also a great system for correction systems and addiction recovery. Entitlement is an addiction. *I used to believe nicotine was the hardest addiction to break. Entitlement is tougher.*

So how do you change from PMO to PCO? This little graphic maps the path.

Confront the facts. Identify where behavioral consequences are missing. Quantify the cost to your organization of death by indecision. Decide which battles you are willing to fight. Any reversal of entitlement will be met with violent resistance and revolt. Better to build with encouragement and consequence systems, but PMO happens. **So be real and be honest.**

Give plenty of lead time to the change but not so much that griping and groaning have time to build barriers. That is a fine balance. Discuss openly before removing entitlement doles. This won't change anything, but it will **establish a new thought pattern** in those affected. It might have been so long since they had positive reward for productivity that they have forgotten what dignity feels like. Entitlement strips dignity and inner drive. **Dignity based on reality has to be instilled fresh**.

Move to consequence and positive reward. You might find this difficult. Your management team may have no idea how to identify positive and productive behavior. They are used to promoting entitlement and systemized to zombie workplace. Dilbert might be their favorite cartoon for a reason. Of course, as the executive leader admit your guilt in leadership. You will have to change, too. The greatest failures of organizations wanting to make this move is that **top leadership credits the workforce for being more powerful than the executives and blames them instead of the mirror**. Truthfully, it takes combined efforts of management and work team to enter entitlement and to exit entitlement.

Measure Shock and Fear. This will be large. Get ready. Get poised. Backbiting, blaming, and bickering will explode. But it will pass if you hold ground. Keep focus on where you are going, encourage the afflicted, and do not let this stop you. If you stop here, you will find it doubly difficult to work on this in the future. Many companies sell out at this point and leave the issues for the new owner. They may scuttle great managers and executives as sacrifices to the masses. **Don't doubt in the dark what you know in the light.** Keep moving forward. Plan to run. Run the plan.

Productive Behavior and Growth. Here is where you land. Here is where you focus. Here is where you want to be. The Positive Change Organization promotes, inspires, and realizes productive behavior and growth. Not everyone can exist in this environment. Yes, you may lose some people you had believed to be key. Not everyone wants to change. Try to salvage them, but don't sink productivity in the process. New leaders will rise. They've been poised for this new environment and potential was shadowed in the old system. Now you can see them.

PMO or PCO? You decide every day with every decision what environment you wish to build.

Enjoy a Better Life Forward. ;-{) phil

Exceptions Are Not Rules: 3 Safe Guards

The life of a manager would not be complete without that wonderful day where she finds herself stumped as to why a staff member acted in a certain manner inconsistent with policy. After several months of training a colleague, you find them going a different direction than guided. It is inevitable. It will happen.

The next surprise is when they tell you it was your idea. What? My idea? What incredible bump do you have on your head that caused such a thought? Have you lost your mind? Where did you get that idea?

Then you remember. You remember the question you answered last week in the middle of a major emergency. A customer needed an exception to your normal policy for a critical project. You authorized the team to process the job in a different manner. It was an exception needed and specific to that day and that job and that customer. Now, it is a rule. Now, it is embedded in the minds of staff as the way to cut a job short.

Of course, if you take this exception route on a routine basis you will lose all your profits, mix up customer work orders, and generally destroy the business. One time on a special project is okay with manager discretion. Any time on normal jobs with a staff discretion is chaos.

Every manager must understand exceptions, communicate them clearly, and contain expanded usage.

The impact of an exception on the minds of team members is big. They watch you, manager. They take clues for action from your action. When you step out of the normal, they believe it is okay to do the same anytime they so choose. Get it? Get it! Guard it.

Understand your own decision. You cannot simply make an exception without understanding and being able to explain to someone else.

Exceptions are not meant to be rules; however, if you don't take the next two steps, they will become rules.

Exceptions will cause a problem. They will. You have order and rules to prevent problems. Okay, accept that and be prepared to contain the problem. Of course, you accommodate for that in your decision. Explain the problem. Explain the accommodation. Explain why this is a onetime decision. Be prepared for questions and distrust. Yes, you worked hard to communicate why you would never do what you just did and then you did it. But, it was an exception, right? You really did have a reason other than you just wanted to do it? Right?

Let your leaders and decision makers know this is an exception, why you made it, and how they might follow your logic in their next decision. Logic? You had some, right?

After an exception, reinforce the rule. Take time to pull documentation if necessary and explain why this is a onetime decision and why not to do it with any regularity. Be honest. Did you do it for political purposes? Then explain the urgency of the situation and protocol you followed. Did you do it to prevent a bigger problem? Don't hide behind, "Because I said so." That is weak and lacks open communication to the team.

Summary: Do these three things when you make an exception and they won't become a rule. Be attentive and cautious when making exceptions that they really fulfill your direction. Always enjoy managing the exceptions and the disciplines.

Enjoy a Better Life Forward. ;-{) phil

{ Understand exceptions

Communicate them clearly

Contain expanded usage. }

Fix the Plumbing

Don't hand your customer toilet paper for a messy problem. Fix the plumbing.

Creative managers create solutions alongside staff. Duct tape and WD40 and vise grips may be all that is needed to do small jobs around the house. That won't do in a productive and viable business. You need to fix the plumbing. You need to eliminate the repeating problem. You need to take responsibility instead of putting the issue in the customer's hands. Don't make them clean it up.

Good service management attends to a few items. There are incidents and service requests, problems and changes. Keep clarity between items. Address appropriately.

Incidents and Service Requests: These two items make up the bulk of customer service.

A service request is what we live to do. A customer asks for a product or service to be delivered. So do it. Do it with excellence and alacrity. Do it with pizzazz and punctuality. Do it. A service request may ask for an altered product or service or a new product or service. That means we have to jump into the area of change and that is another manage well article.

An incident is what we wish would never happen. While delivering a product or service, something is not right. Color is too light. The size is too big. The pizza came with pepperoni instead of black olives. The customer wanted 250 and we delivered 1000. While working with a client, every other email returned an error. My service provider was experiencing incidents. Thankfully they cleared the issue, but not before my customer had to wait extra minutes waiting on reports to be delivered as I had promised. Incidents need to be restored to proper service levels immediately and product or service delivered.

Problems and Changes: Confuse these and your customers will suffer unreasonable delays and constant delivery disruption.

Problems are incidents that won't go away until a change is made. *A fix is just a fancy name for a change.* When the plumbing backed up into my house through the shower drain, it impressed me something was tragically wrong. All the paper towels and mop buckets would not resolve this. When a problems occurs you need to look for root cause of the issue and determine a resolution or change to be made to stop the incidents from coming back. The sewer main had collapsed at the saddle in my back yard blocking all drainage from the house. The city came, sent cameras down the lines, and claimed it was an incident, it was my incident, and they were going home. I don't think so. A friend and I dug seven foot deep in my back yard until we found the collapsed connection leading to the major collapsed connection. The city came back and repaired at much expense and then paid to restore my house to right order. Their paper towel and toilet paper solution was not going to fix my backhoe and major plumbing problem. Full repair and restoration was needed. The root cause had to be determined and a change made to get us back on track.

Changes move the nature of the service into a different order*.* Replacing the main saddle in my back yard not only restored right water flow out of the house, it took care of a sinkhole that could have swallowed one of my children. No one knew the sink hole existed until we dug up the yard. There were bigger problems looming that the change repaired. Changes fix things for good. Not necessarily forever, but for good. And they have potential to adjust the nature of the product or service.

By handing me a toilet paper solution the city was setting us all up for some major pain.

Kudos for the city. The next time I had a city potential issue, the service manager came out, inspected, found a crack in the line feeding water to my house, repaired it, installed a new meter, and made me a happy man. It was a different experience and one for which I am grateful. Oh, they also reversed charges on my water bill even though the leak appeared to be in my pipe not the city pipe. That is service. They took responsibility for a debatable item and went an extra step. I love my city's service.

Summary: Get your customer back to service as rapidly as possible. And then look deeper to determine if a problem exists that will cause service to be impacted again. Find the root and fix the plumbing. Work on your shop processes. Look for machine malfunctions. Examine reporting routines. Do whatever it takes to eliminate repeating incidents. Your customer will appreciate. Your business will grow.

Enjoy a Better Life Forward. ;-{) phil

Presence Communicates Production Priority

Managers and leaders communicate priority by where they spend their time. Production teams make America happen. A walk through a production press room tells the workers they are important and what they do is important. Stopping by the front desk in the morning and looking the receptionist in the eye followed by a specific word of appreciation tells the company that guests are important. Openly discussing decisions and gaining feedback from the team along the way gives them a stake. Presence communicates production priority.

30 years of overseeing production teams 24/7 leaves me with a little insight on helping a shift through their day. Every shift is a day in itself. Each one needs right attention and priority.

Every meeting you attend, every walk down the hallway, every lunch in public communicates your deepest heart. You are being watched. An encouraging word, a kind action, opening a door for someone else, or a playful interchange all communicate compassion and priority.

An ancient proverb tells us to not muzzle the oxen as they tread grain. One visual picture we draw is of an ox pulling along in a field being harvested. He needs to munch a little every once in a while. He needs to gain benefit while working, not just at the end of the season. Your presence and encouragement is one of the daily benefits you can give with little cost and great results. Corporate parties, big meetings and bonuses help. They can never replace personal attention and involvement. Presence communicates production priority every day and communicates concern for the people.

Early in the Day Sets a Tone
A manager starts the day for work teams. A little whistle up the hallway in the morning tells the team it is a bright day. Pleasant greetings communicate positive expectation and confidence. It is not just physical presence but emotional engagement that builds a productive team of individuals bound by mission.

Middle of the Day Stimulates
By mid-day in a production crew, sales team, customer service group, or any other set of individuals bound by mission, there have been problems. Opportunity to turn dour has come many times by noon. This is one perfect moment to inspire and prioritized. Where you spend the last minutes before lunch tells the team where to focus.

A purposeful and thoughtful communication to key team members on priority projects can keep problems from dominating. Customer service needs to keep moving while issues are resolved. Down equipment needs attended. Production schedules may need adjusted considering current availability. Sales teams may need a pep talk to overcome any weight of complaints.

End of the Day Rules over Tides
By the end of a good day, there have been powerful moments and struggling moments. Tides have pressed against the team attempting to bring them to defeat. They need presence. They need reinforcement that the customer is king and the team is in your heart. You need to let them know you are on their side. Before you go home, visit the oncoming team and give them the same whistling start you gave the first team.

Summary: Presence communicates production priority. Production is the ox of your company. Sales must happen. Production must run seamless. An ancient proverb tells us to not muzzle the ox as he treads the grain. Consider your time and attention and presence as un-muzzling the oxen. Invest in your people. They are the strength of the company.

The Road to Human Loyalty- A Forever Journey

"Life does not consist mainly, or even largely, of facts and happenings. It consists mainly of the storm of thought that is forever flowing through one's head." Mark Twain

Greatness finds ways to be loyal and extract loyalty from those they serve. It is reciprocal. It is not a given.

Goodness find ways to give and earn respect.

Mediocrity finds ways to get by and fill the role.

You want loyalty above respect. You want to live in greatness. You can live in mediocrity or goodness or greatness. Choose.

Greatness: Every human relationship has the potential to be a great relationship. A customer can be a great customer. A supporter can be a great supporter. A family member can be a great family member. A co-worker can be a great co-worker. A staff member can be a great staff member. Choose. The choice lies in the hands of whoever takes the lead. Lead well. Manage that relationship.

Stages: There are five discernible stages to an effective relationship. Fringe, friend, familiar, faithful, and forever. You may have more, but I find these cross most relationships. In non-profits and congregations, I add a few and change the names around. These five hold. Honor them in building service inside your organization and amazing results transpire.

Fringe: Every relationship starts on the fringe. These are people with whom you have no relationship at all. They do not even know you exist. You may not know they exist. They are out there waiting to get to know you and enjoy your companionship and possibly your service. Respect them as valuable. Honor them. Give them credit for being worthy of dignity and your attention. People are worthy of your attention.

Friend: Somewhere you meet. Someone visits your brick and mortar shop. You talk to a businessman about a new sign. At the bank, you open a new account and meet a representative. Each human transaction can open a friendship. They become more aware of you and you become more aware of them. Being a friend is more than just acquaintance. You exchange information about each other. This exchange opens the next path. Many businesses leave potential customers at this juncture. They know your name and your business but nothing about you and your mission and vision and hopes and dreams and likes and dislikes. Open up and develop this relationship.

Familiar: Now, you have transacted business. This may be with a staff member where you've worked on a project. It could be with a customer who has purchased product or service. Maybe you have participated in a class discussion. But, there has been significant exchange requiring trust and revealing of more information. The familiar are more likely to engage at continuing intimacy of relationship and trust. Most people stop in relationships at this level. Customers never become settled. Staff members are held at a distance. Co-workers struggle to fully understand each other.

DANGER! The next two levels are dangerous. They require open-hearted exposure. That is why most never enter into these levels. When you lose a relationship at one of these levels it is painful. To be great, you must risk and receive pain. Go for it. The pleasure of good customer and co-worker relationships at these levels outweigh the pain. Assess the ability to be loyal in customers before you move them up into these ranks. Some customers are just jerks. Sorry. Be cautious. Some supporters are over controlling. Don't be a fool and risk your organization. Some co-workers need psychologists more than you need them to get too close to the knitting. Advance the best and honor the rest.

Faithful: Over time, the familiar enter into more and more transactions. They become faithful. A faithful customer orders over and over. A faithful co-worker takes and gives advice continually and participates in more and more projects and actions. A faithful supporter reads updates and gives regularly. There is a goodwill and loyalty exchange that has become a given in the relationship.

Forever: Few relationships reach this level. There is a foundational commitment and insider understanding of operations for a business. These are customers for life. You find yourself talking through key business strategies with a foundational customer. A foundational co-worker sees you at your worst and at your best. A foundational supporter in a non-profit understands the mix of vision and mission and can advise on action with your best interest at heart.

Movement: Advancing from fringe to forever should be a pathway for marketing, operations, and activities of any organization. Take time to understand the events, education, information, engagement, transaction, and social touches that assist customers, co-workers, and compatriots in moving along this path. Each of these paths is a continual exchange and deepening of relationship. None should be one way. Have a purposeful plan to advance the best of the best relationships into the Forever circle.

Summary: This is a quick caricature of a complicated subject. Take time to map out your advancement strategies especially with key stakeholders and players in your life. You can have some wonderful moments with Forever people as customers, co-workers, and compatriots.

Remember people are not static. As much as you invest, at any time an individual may abort the relationship and move to a conflict level or vacate the relationship. That is a risk. But the joy of good connections outweigh the risks.

Enjoy a Better Life Forward. ;-{) phil

Vacation Reverses Progress: Reinforce Routines on Return

After a few days of rest, the human mind plays an ornery trick on managers. Staff members have a frustratingly human characteristic of change reversal. Ignore it and you will continually lose ground. Leadership management considers this rule and makes adjustments to reduce impact.

Here is the rule: Humans tend to revert to the deeply ingrained pattern of behavior that existed prior to the last major change under stress, duress, or rest.

Here is an example: Manager X implemented a new routine for checking work quality in line with the process in March. The results have been good. All staff have adapted and are working under the new approach. Prior to this, many production orders had to be returned to the beginning and rebuilt. The shop standard had been to only check product at time of packing and shipping. Problems at this point required many hours to fix and a great waste in complete orders produced multiple times. The changes implemented to utilize steering controls along the production path had resulted in an 80% reduction in waste as problems were caught in time to correct and make adjustments along the path.

Over the July 4th holiday, many staff members took extra days of vacation and enjoyed themselves immensely. Manager X was surprised and happy to see the team enjoy time with family and friends and morale looked better than in years. But, waste was creeping back up to last year levels and customers were complaining of late orders. On a walk-through, it was obvious that a few of the colleagues were not performing the steering controls that had been implemented and stabilized into the production process. In fact, it seemed that every staff member was skipping some control point at random. The team had reverted to depending on the last check point to catch errors before they impacted the customer.

This was not a purposeful sabotage. This was human nature. Upon return from vacations, orders had picked up. Customers came back from vacation with a backlog of rush orders. Suppliers were slow with needed inventory. The new production checkpoint pattern had not had time to fully integrate into a subconscious activity. The team had been good at performing, but had not subconsciously integrated the process. That takes many months. Each person had reverted to a different pattern of work that was a mishmash of prior procedure and present process.

What to Do? An astute manager is aware of this phenomenon. School systems are working to address this across the United States. They notice students returning from summer vacations seem to have lost major portions of knowledge they had been taught in the last semester. Some schools have shortened summer to attempt to address. They may find that the amount of time off consolidated may have little effect on the phenomena. The biggest effect is brain rest and disconnect. That can happen in a few days. The difference between one month and three months is probably negligible. But, what does a manager do? How can he or she keep production running smooth?

1. Get ahead of the vacation curve. Right before a major holiday make a concerted effort to reinforce training on any critical changes made within four months of the holiday. Bring it fresh to mind and communicate priority immediately before vacation.

2. Notice those on your team that do this most frequently. Spend some time with them on return from vacation or other time off to reinforce changes. Give them time to ask questions and rethink through routines before they run back to the production floor. If you can't pull them away, at least show up at their workstation and ask how the modified routines are working. Put priority on the changes by asking questions about them.

3. Don't use banners or wall posters or email to get this job done. Get personal. Presence communicates priority. Your face and voice in the mix will mean a lot and can do a lot to stir good adherence to right routine. Those other methods are okay to reinforce personal involvement, but will never get the job done by themselves.

4. Consider holidays into project plans when implementing major changes. Don't put a change into place too close to a holiday. Make sure major changes are implemented at least two to three months prior to big holidays, when you know you will have many staff members taking time away from the job. Give people time to integrate change before the rest periods.

Summary: Managers manage change. There are rules of change that are attached to human nature. Ignore them at great pain. Acknowledge them and see better results in your teams.

Enjoy a Better Life Forward. ;-{) phil

Reasonable Price and Trusted Service

If I can do this for a reasonable price, will you do the business with me?

The executive and manager establish thought pattern and policy among service and sales and customer. Go for reasonable price business. The bid mentality prevalent in many industries is predicated on being short changed in a transaction. Reasonable price is predicated on trust, loyalty, and commitment to the good of the customer. Over time, a reasonable price relationship delivers the best product for a customer at the best price. Excess people time, unwanted and mismatched goods and services and mistakes decrease. Major cost savings are engaged.

Meet A Need: Ask this question when working with "bid" mentality buyers before you haggle on pennies. The question digs to the real trust involved in the transaction. The question reveals your heart to do the best work for the client at a reasonable cost according to their needs.

Ask this question when working with a trusted client, who has come to you with a bid.

Rule of Respect: Ask this question as a rule of respect and many clients will engage business with you based on trust and your commitment to reasonable pricing and exceptional service. Both of you will save money as trust is a faster transaction, requires less people involved on both ends, and over time ends up in a continuing lowering of cost based on watching out for the good of your client.

Are You Being Real? Are you coming to me with this business in order to justify an action with someone else on which you have already decided? Are you bringing this to me as an honest opportunity with a fair chance for me to do the business? Do I have a chance to establish a trusted relationship with you for other business?

Are You Still With Me? For the existing client, this could lead to other questions. Maybe they have lost some trust due to a miscommunication. Maybe someone has opened a question in their mind about you and your team that needs answered. Maybe they are just feeling a little neglected or want to express some freedom. It is worth asking.

Engage The Heart of Service: Many internal organization providers look to get "right of first refusal" or "right to do business within a fixed percentage". It amounts to the same question *only if your heart of service is fully engaged*. If you are looking to force someone to do business with you through top down edict, they will mistrust you and find an alternate path. Frustration and lack of liberty in decision making breeds corruption and creative means of policy avoidance.

Reality Check: One client continually asked for pricing. This habit was costing us and them. The cost of estimating many times was more than the total price of the transaction. They were losing money bidding the items and we were losing money estimating minute work orders. Our customer service team engaged the "reasonable price" approach. Since the customer was familiar with our pricing through many transactions, they began to say yes. This alone cut four or five phone calls out of each transaction. Then they just moved to ordering with reasonable price expectation. This cut hours of their time and our time out of each order and moved orders into the production queue many days faster as approvals accompanied the initial request. People focused on quality and clarity and exactness in delivery instead of pennies. This customer is a customer for life in a trusted relationship based on reasonable price.

The 3 Questions

Bring a team into high productivity and positive morale with "The 3 Questions". Managers must master these. Imbed them into your psyche. Repeat them in your sleep. Make them your meditational mantra. Get it.

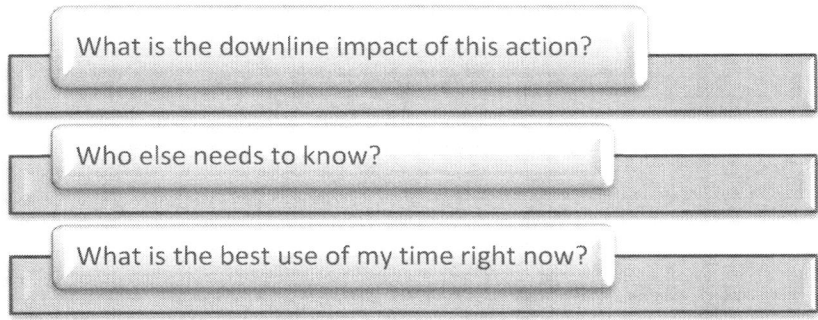

What is the down-line impact of this action? How often do you have problems in production or sales or finance because of an inadequate exploration of this question? What will happen in accounting if we promote this new product line at 5% markdown? What will happen to other product lines? Can marketing adjust in time for the sales season? Will production be ready to handle sales volumes?

Put off this question at maximum risk of failure. Even the simplest action in a sequence of workflow has to pursue an expanded understanding before change. If we print this at a new size, will the finishing team be able to handle it? If we promote a new advantage to our product will it meet compliance guidelines? When we implement this change to our computer program for billing will it cause extra workload at 3am that affects another unrelated cycle? There is no end to implications of one actions on other team action. No one can know them all. But you need to ask.

Who else needs to know? How familiar is your team with the interaction of what they do with others? Do you have workers living in a vacuum? Have you taken time to educate them about interplay with other departments, people, teams, divisions, customers, and vendors? When you change the usage of a machine, it might be wise to include the manufacturer in the discussion. Ask often, "Who else needs to know?"

What is your information plan to include them? When do they need to know? Do they have access to enhanced information that might help you make a better decision before advancing?

Work with a production team with large dependency on delivery cycles proved out value here. The delivery team was constantly a day behind. They were only being informed at the time of pickup. By moving the information to them at time of beginning of production, a day was cut out of delivery cycle to the customer and orders increased with increased customer satisfaction. The sales team also needed to know at the same time instead of being informed only after delivery. This enabled them to engage the customer along the path with pertinent and reliable information. Who else needs to know?

What is the best use of my time right now? After you ask the first two questions, answer this one. Too often we ask this one and answer it only considering what we know and what we are doing. We need to consider what others know and what they are doing. A project launch could falter due to conflicting priorities in the organization. A customer order may not be deliverable as requested due to a supply shortage and should be renegotiated. After considering the plans and availabilities of others and related resources, we may want to work on an entirely different project or action and time this one in front of us into another day or week.

Summary Simplicity: These 3 questions are priceless practice for any manager for self-decisions and for training team members in their decisions. After working with a team for a season on these, you will find they become masters of the top manager rule. What is the top manager rule? NO SURPRISES. These questions eliminate the element of surprise and provide a foundation for a self-managed team.

Enjoy a Better Life Forward. ;-{) phil

Ask them often.

What is the down-line impact of my action?

Who else needs to know?

What is the best use of my time right now?

Be Busy Building Better Business,

Renaissance Man – There is No Box

Danny DeVito starred in an acclaimed movie entitled, Renaissance Man. He impacted others to believe outside the restrictions of present systems. My junior year of university, Dean Musselman tagged me with that title. As he reviewed my business, psychology, literature, religion, and sociology mix of courses, he both scratched his balding dome and complimented me for being broad in my quest for understanding.
Renaissance leads to revelation. **There is no box.**

Wikipedia defines the Renaissance Man as
"A polymath (Greek: πολυμαθής, *polymathēs*, "having learned much"), is a person whose **expertise spans a significant number of different subject areas**; such a person is known to draw on complex bodies of knowledge to solve specific problems"

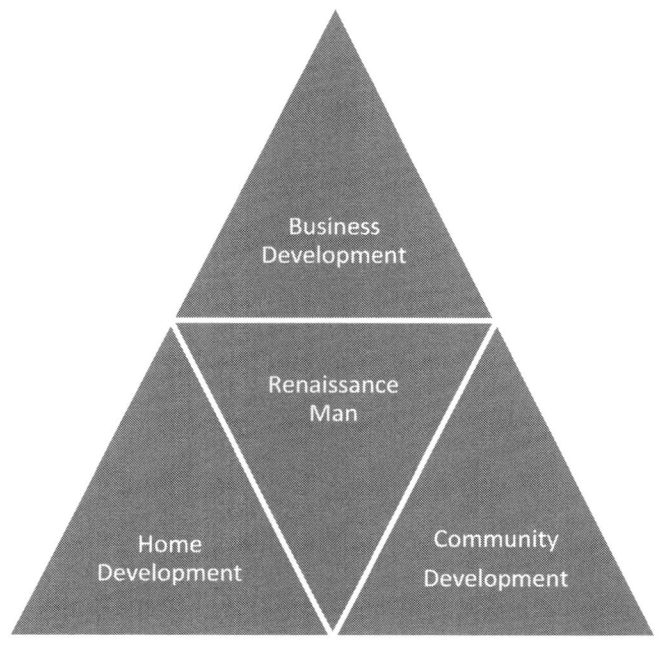

My personal form comes in taking a few keen skills honed over many iterations in business, community, and congregation and offer them to you. Most of us in our journeys do not discover who we really can be until later in life. Some find the path early. Finding an early path to late discovery is a joy.

Excellence in operations and communications really shouts what I want to say to you. Business, community, and home are fields of prosperity. Leadership in community (business, government, education, non-profit), leadership in the people services (non-profit, congregation) and leadership in the home (fathers and families) build the environment in which healthy, dedicated, morally and emotionally and socially competent individuals and groups develop in balance and holistic health.

Where Are You? Every individual needs to discover the "out of box" experience. Who are you? As a leader and manager, you cannot exclude yourself from life. The balance of who you are impacts every action from attending a sports event to playing with your kids to sitting in a meeting at the office.

Enjoy a Better Life Forward. ;-{) phil

Razor Sharp Relationships – 10 Risk Taker Tips

Every executive, director, manager and minion is tasked with developing increasing levels of intimacy in right service relationships. Intimacy? Yes. A satisfied customer can become a delighted customer. A satisfied customer can become a dissatisfied customer. An emotionally distant and dissatisfied customer is on the way to another shop. A customer, who is an intimate associate, will stay with you and work through dissatisfaction. So how do you move customers from fringe relationships to intimate foundational associates?

This note comes as a response to a client question. His particular struggle was intimacy with clients. That is a tough subject. Most of us like to separate our business relationships into a compartment of mistrust. "Caveat vendor" and "Caveat emptor" pervade. Getting to **a trusted win-win relationship** confidence assumption requires exposure and intimacy and increasing levels of personal revelation. Sound risky? It is. Risk brings reward.

TRUST = RISK = GROWTH

A good friend in the business took me into his back office and showed me a project recently that is a **highly competitive move** for him. He exposed himself. He knows I also work with his competitors. Trust means I can do a better job helping him as I understand his needs and focus. Trust means no one knows but me what I saw.

With one client, when I took an antagonistic department head into the inner workflow of the shop, I was frozen with fear. Surely they would tear the client apart in front of some executive over a small disagreement of approach. On the contrary, they reciprocated and let me into their workflow. We built a **cooperative system of workflow** that ended up in our locking shop and customer into a 100% provider relationship.

Another client took me into their private conference room with a group of key decision makers. This was a **culturally and politically tense** situation. Without trust and intimacy this discussion would be over before we started. The executive could lose a lot of face if I did not relate to each person in the group well. She was staking business strategy for the next three years on this discussion. The pressure was on. In a few minutes one of the key stakeholders and I discovered a common interest in the field we were discussing and the group took off into a vibrant and open discussion.

"We judge ourselves by our intentions and others by their behavior." Stephen M.R. Covey, The SPEED of Trust: The One Thing that Changes Everything

Developing successful relationships from fringe to friend to familiar to faithful to forever is a principle I work to instill in every organization. It is **The Road to Human Loyalty**. It applies to staff relationships and customer relationships and community relationships. There are a few "caveats" in this path and you need to take time to understand them, but they are deeper than starting out with a lack of trust.

So as you work on your plans for the next 18 months and consider your customer relationships here are a few tips. Sure you will meet some disappointments when you apply them. However, you will find you gain much more than you lose.

1. Take time to listen deeply and unplug the filters of prior expectation.
2. Be slow to judge motivations for the heart is a complicated web.
3. Give yourself 20 seconds to consider and weigh before you respond to any situation.
4. Reaction to medicine will kill you. Response will heal you. Choose response.
5. The space between stimulus and response is filled by choice.
6. Believe in your customer.
7. Believe in yourself.
8. Think of ten good actions you could take in response to a request before making a decision when feeling like you are being used.
9. If you consider all your relationships as well, think again and be realistic.
10. Do the thing you fear the most, give trust.

Enjoy a Better Life Forward. ;-{) phil

4 As of Team: Identify Structure

Teamwork is not simple and not common. A well-functioning team is powerful and poised for growth. Why do you allow areas of your company to operate with dysfunction? Do you realize the power of synergy you lose? Great teams have accountability, adherence, action, and alliance knit into performance and decisions. To adopt the Four As of Team identify where you are. Executives must lead.

For the past 33 years, I have looked in the mirror every morning and asked myself: 'If today were the last day of my life, would I want to do what I am about to do today?' And whenever the answer has been 'No' for too many days in a row, I know I need to change something.
Steve Jobs

- Command and Control
- Laissez Faire
- Helicopter Micro Manager
- Staff Rules
- Courage and Consequence

Command and Control: This can be good practice in crisis and creation. But, it does not resemble team. A command and control structure with hierarchical dictates allows for quick obedience. It also promotes mindless action. You had better be ready to lose thoughtful workers. This is great in a battlefield of well-defined parameters. It is death when you need mental acuity and engaged creativity.

Laissez Faire: Apathetic management will render apathetic results. How often have you found a manager so afraid of making mistakes that decisions linger? Indecision runs rampant and results wander further off target over time. Many times this is symptomatic of Command and Control structure in the higher hierarchy. Managers freeze because they know every decision is really made in an upper level and they have no authority, just responsibility. And that is a disease, not a management practice. Team? Not on your life. Everyone lives for himself. Finger pointing and blame shifting become survival necessities.

Helicopter Micro Management: Wow. This one is painful for every worker. Authority to make decisions may be released, but any small mistake is noted and put into the brown stamp book for later redemption. This environment breeds anger. Rewards are rare except to the micro manager, who redeems all the good points for her own benefit. There might be a team of workers gelled to mutinous intent. This is common in highly political organizations.

Staff Rules: This dysfunctional team approach is gaining ground in many organizations. Executives, directors, and managers are afraid of the employees. What if they don't like me and my vision? What if they go somewhere else? What if they file a complaint with HR? What if, what if, and what if cause managers to check in with employees on every decision. This is entitlement mentality and will lower and lower productivity to the level of the most charismatic laggard in the shop. The danger is that managers believe this will improve morale. The exact opposite is true. People thrive on leadership that is decisive, non-political, visionary, supportive, and fair. It is not fair to allow the least productive the same reward as the most productive in a free market economy. The dichotomy of this approach is that executives begin making hidden decisions because it is impossible to please everyone. So really, you are living in Command and Control with a ruse of inclusion.

Courage and Consequence: The best team structure rewards both courage and consequence. There is a reward system for the over achievers. There is a consequence system for the under achievers. It may not be money. It may be getting more training or being included on key work teams or allowance for a flexible schedule or whatever works for the producer. Isn't that going to be interpreted as "teacher's pet" activity? Sure. Deal with it. That is the courage part. Courage starts with the executive and director.

It may be hard for an egg to turn into a bird: it would be a jolly sight harder for it to learn to fly while remaining an egg. We are like eggs at present. And you cannot go on indefinitely being just an ordinary, decent egg. We must be hatched or go bad. C. S. Lewis

Summary: Identify your team. Where are you? How did you get there? Is it where you want it? In the next idea I address the As of accountability and adherence that make a powerful and productive team. You cannot afford to lag in the first four structures. Neither can you change overnight. I'll give you solid tips on making transitions built over time and tension and triumph.

Enjoy a Better Life Forward. ;-{) phil

4 As of Team: Accountability and Adherence

Identification of the most **common team structure** (*Read prior chapter.*) allows you to define the beginning steps toward the productive and pleasant work environment you desire. It won't be easy. Shop mentalities build over time. They don't change overnight. They don't change without strong resistance. Resistance is not a bad item. It just is. Change is painful. Who wants pain? You do. You must change to reach the place of pleasant productivity you crave. There is a freedom in a productive team that makes life enjoyable.

Change does not roll in on the wheels of inevitability, but comes through continuous struggle. And so we must straighten our backs and work for our freedom. A man can't ride you unless your back is bent. Martin Luther King, Jr.

Courage and Consequence			
Accountability	Adherence	Action	Alliance

Courage and Consequence: This is the team you want. Empowered staff makes good decisions, takes good action, thinks good thoughts, embraces excellence in operations, and follows right process and procedure and policy. Wow? Who is in charge of this utopia? You are. Vision, mission, and plans guide accomplishment of key organizational objectives. It is achievable, enjoyable, and realistic.

Accountability: Absent in many teams is fair accountability. Sure, you might have erratic accountability or skewed accountability, but do you have fair accountability? Fair accountability includes up-to-date job descriptions with room for growth. Fair accountability includes up-to-date shop policy and procedure and processes with identified measurements of success at low, medium and high levels. Fair accountability includes allowances for exceptions with appropriate discretionary latitude at the lowest point of decision making. Fair accountability includes identifiable career path.

Adherence: Alongside accountability is adherence to policy and procedure. When the accountability lies outside the individual team member for her actions you find shop standards slipping, waste unacceptable, and constant angst with little improvement. Why adhere to procedure if no one cares or checks equitably? You need firm adherence to clear and communicated process, policy, and procedure to run alongside accountability.

Check Up on Accountability:

Plus Checks: Are all key shop processes identified and process owners acknowledged and empowered? Are all procedures up-to-date with present software, equipment, and expected people skills? Is there a skills inventory and signoff by responsible staff for each process for which they are responsible? Do you have a training plan for each member of the team for cross training and extra support?

Minus Checks: Are staff members allowed to continually bypass procedures during "hot" jobs? Do you have known team members who are incompetent in some assigned duties required for their role? Are some team members constantly covering for others?

Transition Approaches for Each Dysfunction to Courage and Consequence:

Command and Control: Begin with a process inventory. Identify team members who will be owners of each process. Require delegation with increasing levels of responsibility for procedures and policies. This will start the communication to the entire team that you are serious.

Laissez Faire: Begin with procedures. Identify consequences to customers of not following the flow. Managers communicate to the team the impact on customers in a matter of fact manner. Begin to win their hearts to service.

Helicopter Micro Management: Begin with results reports for feedback. Pull back the micro manger one key result at a time. Implement 10-2-4 checks against reasonable expectations that are results oriented not operation oriented. Make sure your customers get good work while decreasing oversite of mundane tasks.

Staff Rules: When coming from Staff Rules begin with procedures created by the staff. Don't rob them of power. Focus their energy. Identify process owners who are final signoff on procedures in their areas. Delegate clearly and communicate changes to the entire team in person where possible and by email only in emergencies.

You must be the change you wish to see in the world.
Mahatma Gandhi

Fear Factors: Moving into accountability and adherence in a shop increases fear. The prior system is predictable. People fear losing predictability. They greatly fear being held accountable until they experience living with it and receiving results. Fear can result in many types of resistance. "No one ever told me." "Who made that decision?" "That's not what I read." "_____ is responsible." "That's not the job I was hired to do." As an executive, director, or manager, you have to provide clear, communicated, and consistent response to these reactions to slowly eliminate fear. It will rise. You need to manage the fear without retreat.

4 As of Team: Action and Alliance

Find productivity improvements, lower risk and reduce expenses with 4A teams. A good team gives bottom line results consistently and with increasing customer satisfaction.   Give managers support from the top to make this happen. In the first article (**Identify Structure**) positive and negative approaches are identified. In the second (Accountability and Adherence) the priority pair of As are outlined. Now let's deliver the goods. Action and Alliance build team synergy.

Courage and Consequence			
Accountability	Adherence	Action	Alliance

Action: Teams need action.   Teams need people of action. Issues erupt. Machines fail. There is no greater pain than walking into a shop that is inactive for hours due to fear of action. Costly hours have been spent with no product to show. Somebody said he would do what she wouldn't and nobody moved. Inaction is death to excellence. Dysfunctional team structure will exacerbate inaction. Courage and consequence stirs action mode team.

Free action requires empowerment. Right process and policy and procedure give each team member clear expectations and parameters for decisions to achieve organization objectives. If staff needs to consult a manager more than once a week, empowerment is weak.

Alliance: Build key alliances with vendors, suppliers, departments, team members, and customers. Alliances require maintenance. Build trust and tenacity. Never assume loyalty. Strengthen understanding and alliance with allowance for mistakes. High accountability affords grace for mistakes. Do not allow ignorance of the needs of partners and stakeholders.

Check Up on Action and Alliance:

Plus Checks: When team members are proactive are they given immediate and specific feedback? Is proactive approach on every personnel review? Do leadership team meetings include kudos for proactive solutions attributed to team members? Is there an active and up-to-date list of alliance vendors, suppliers, and customers published to the leadership group with assigned action quarterly for communication? Do you have fun events with partners and stakeholders? Do alliances know your strategic objectives for the next 18 months?

Minus Checks: Are team members ignorant of business impact of product and services on the end customer of your customer? Is a clear customer communication process of risk of missing due times integrated into every team member's expectations? Do team members hesitate to make decisions when management is out of office?

Transition Approaches for Each Dysfunction to Courage and Consequence:

Command and Control: Establish "do then report" into a few key activities. Review your process flow for steering points where decisions can branch to failure and embed a manager call out into the routine. Over time reduce these points with coaching.

Laissez Faire: Explain the business impact of the end customer of the customer to all team members. Make this a part of your management communiqués and public interaction. Establish "down line impact" mentality. Help each person see the impact of their action on the next person in the process stream.

Helicopter Micro Management: Back off. Get out of the way. Identify where you need proactive small steps and find ways to compliment. Focus on progress toward the end goal instead of the end goal. Read a book on positive reinforcement theory and adjust your attitude.

"Trust is the glue of life. It's the most essential ingredient in effective communication. It's the foundational principle that holds all relationships." — Stephen R. Covey

Staff Rules: Establish clear vision, mission, and 18 month objectives. Communicate, communicate, and communicate. Establish buy-in. Don't do this quickly. Lock yourself out and get a vision, plan, and timeline in your heart and mind. Discuss with the key influencers of the team. Establish lost leadership. Bring firm vision for their discussion.

When we are no longer able to change a situation – we are challenged to change ourselves. Viktor E. Frankl

Summary: Action and alliance build a synergistic environment. Big progress is made. Team finds solutions to long term issues on their own. Plaguing process glitches go away. Responsible behavior now is the norm. Joy takes over. Move into 4 As Team. Do it.

Enjoy a Better Life Forward. ;-{) phil

Training Tenacity

Exerting your vision through your people and customers requires training. You need to train team. You need to train prospects and customers. You need to train yourself. You need to train your board. You must perform with consistency, congruency, and tenacity. They may resist. Do it anyway.

Train Your Team

Customer Service: A relaxed customer service is failure in the making. Many inside service teams unravel at this point. Every team member must understand the vision of the service group. They must breathe it and live it. It should affect every point of decision.

TRAINING			
Team	Customers	Self	Board

Let's use a print operation as an example. In a print plant, the press tech, the manager, the finishing tech, the shipping clerk, and the prepress tech must breathe customer service. Every type operation has similar roles. This means constant training on phone skills, face-face consistency, issue handling, and prioritization to customer need. How often do decisions get made based on equipment and supplies versus customer demand? Change it. Attend to it always.

Customer Knowledge: Teams need to know who they serve. Communicate personal information about the key customers. Did someone recently have a baby? Take a once in a life time trip? Accomplish a certification? Why do you restrict this knowledge to the sales and customer service teams? When your team members know the customers they serve in simple ways, they take what they do more personal and increase excellence.

Team Technical: All falls apart if the machines are not running. Machines run with good files, good process, and good people. Good people are trained. They are retrained. They are over trained.

Train Your Customer

"Personally, I'm always ready to learn, although I do not always like being taught." Sir Winston Churchill, British Prime Minister

Mission Critical: Customers must be trained. Men and women around the world follow leadership into life ending battles. They grasp a purpose, attach to leadership, and thrust themselves into the oncoming firestorm. Your customers have a mission purpose. When you show them how their mission purpose connects with your service, you gain customers for life. They want to have loyal and mission attached service and will fight through budgets, purchasing departments, discretionary funds, and idiosyncrasies of their organization to work with you. Connect them. Educate them.

Linked Process: Customer process must be engaged. Discover their process and adapt yours to work with theirs. Educate them on your journey and your excellence. Take time to make them more knowledgeable on your ordering and delivering process than you are. They don't care how you print it. They care how you interact with them at beginning and end of process. The better they understand, the easier their life becomes and the more they turn to you for service with a smile.

Train Yourself

Be the expert in your industry. Know substrates and capabilities and twenty uses for every machine.

Be the expert in your people. Learn something new every day about a team member. Surprise yourself.

Be the expert in your customers. Study their needs and demands. Know what they need before they know what they need.

Be the expert in your customers industry. Read industry articles and journals your customers read. Get outside your pocket of knowledge.

Be the expert in the mundane. Maybe the numbers don't excite you. Maybe organization process is boring. Master the mundane. Take a college course. Go interview an executive or manager in another area of the organization and learn what they know.

Train the Board

There are executive stakeholders surrounding every decision you make. Official or unofficial, you have a stakeholder board. They may meet in a room or in the hallway. Get them trained. Keep them updated with quick, pithy mission points of accomplishment and plans. Let them be involved in your decision thinking. You may not have an official board of advisors, but you better have a list for your own reference.

Summary: This is quick and high level. Every organization must train these four and train them well. Skip one and risk failure. Tend to all and move forward. Overcome your inertia. Move on it.

Enjoy a Better Life Forward. ;-{) phil

The Fearful and the Brave

Pursuing growth takes courage. The brave take bold steps. Every executive, director and manger come to moments of decision. Some require bravery. Some require casting off fear. A brave decision maker in the print business must know three things.

"I find the great thing in this world is not so much where we stand, as in what direction we are moving – we must sail sometimes with the wind and sometimes against it – but we must sail, and not drift, nor lie at anchor." — Oliver Wendell Holmes Sr.

Where are you going? Columbus was a brave soul. He cast off the shore of mediocrity and embarked into an historical trip. His bravery took him and his team into uncharted waters. As a decision maker for one or multiple companies, you need to do the same.

- ***Where is the industry?*** You need to know. What is growing and what is lagging? How will that affect your clients and prospects? What do you need to learn to move forward? What do you need to jettison to keep alive? Be bold.

- ***Where is your niche?*** Is it growing? Is it growing in volume, complexity, confluence with related service and product, or number of potential clients? Is it shrinking? Do you need to make a bold strike to hold market share or to improve market position? Be bold.

- ***Where is your risk?*** Can your team keep up the pace? Are they learning at a fast enough rate? Is your equipment and software set where it needs to be? What is your competition doing to put you out of business? Are you poised to meet the challenges? Be bold.

- ***Who is going with me?*** All of us need to sort through good and not-so-good clients.

    - ***Some clients are dragging bottom***. They are anchors on a sailing ship. Every Friday at 2pm they bring impossible requests and frustrate your team on their way to anticipated family time. They call your top sales members in the evening when they would rather be watching a child's soccer game. Files are never ready and cost you more dollars to fix than the profit on the order. Inventory your clients. Can you contain the anchors so they don't damage progress for everyone? Is there a way to manage them and keep the ship running across the ocean at high speed? Be brave.

    - ***Some clients bring valued cargo into the hold.*** Every order is ready to go, priorities are understood, and expectations are in line with your capabilities. You love to meet these folks for lunch and talk about the victories. Profit margins are ample because speed of trust enables lean operation on the orders. Payments or allocations are handled posthaste and receivables look wonderful to your accounting. Be brave.

    - ***Some clients sharpen your saw***. No one shaves off fear quicker than these clients. No one creates fear faster than these clients. Every month, they have a new idea that challenges your team to move faster, brighter, and with more creativity. You love them and hate them. You would never grow without them for they point out the future of the industry. Just when you are comfortable using your wide format for a steady stream of poster orders, this client is ready to print 10,000 labels at high quality with a 48 hour turn. They don't bring an order, they bring ten orders on the same day that utilized 90% of your team's capability. They make you shine. Be brave.

What will we find when we get there?

Contentment lies not in quality or rest, but confidence that what we have done and where we have gone is the right journey. Decision makers pursue contentment not satisfaction. There is a constant dissatisfaction with status quo that drives the bold to stay bold and the brave to be more courageous. Are you dissatisfied enough to be bold?

Summary: Fear stifles and strangles. Bravery shifts and shapes. Take inventory on your plans to ensure they break the boundaries of fear and launch you into the future. You own the future. Serving inside the corporation or company or institution can breed fear. Surrounded by fearful managers looking for the safe route home? Take the lead. Be one of the brave.

Enjoy a Better Life Forward. ;-{) phil

> *Contentment lies not in quality or rest, but confidence that what we have done and where we have gone is the right journey.*

Solving Workflow with Leadership

Quality is best managed by leadership.

The conversation with a commercial manager of multiple in-plants was revelatory. His responsibility covered a variety of situations of business and higher education where management had been sourced. Each instance had a mix of team members who were employees of the institution or business and team members working for the commercial sourcing group. Few of us ever have to work in such a complexity. One of the shops experiences continual quality issues. What is promised and proofed sometimes does not match what is delivered in color consistency. Every shop has to solve this in their workflow. Yet, no shop can ever claim to have final resolution. Why?

Can quality be 100% managed by workflow? Policy and procedure and process never resolve every issue. It is the team member performing the task that must apply discretion and excellence. Machines glitch. Chemical mixes fail. Papers absorb and dissipate moisture. Files are changed two seconds before a run. People forget to communicate changes. All of these items impact workflow. The finest workflow fit to the greatest team and equipment and software and supplies does not accommodate for all variances or all combinations of variances.

Priority and pressure pre-empt. They do. An angry customer can fluster the best of press operators. A haggard executive can shift priorities on a job in process in order to take care of the urgent. When the job is restarted not all the conditions are the same. What was going to be on time is now threatened as a rush. Content may shift due to final edits and the customer overlooks the slight but critical impact on the final piece as they sign the proof and rush out the door at 4:30pm for a piece due the next morning. "Well you signed it!" just does not please the customer after they have handed out the goof at their most important meeting of the month.

Quality is best managed by leadership. Some things are taught and some things are caught. Leadership is best taught by being caught. A production team will reflect the tenor and approach of the leader. If you'd like to have impeccable workflow then start with impeccable leadership. What you do in the shadows will be done in the light. How you handle decisions needing discretion will lead them when you are not there.

Proactive: Leadership looks beyond the specific request to the heart of the need. Instead of overlooking a mistake on a proof by a customer, a leader reviews with the customer and asks qualifying questions if something seems amiss. That is caught when a manager does an employee review or barters with a vendor or approves a request for time off. Do you give that example at all times? Then expect team members to apply during production.

Responsible: Leadership is ownership. A leader will listen to a dissatisfied customer, personally apologize whether involved in the job or not, and give a reliable expectation of correction. That is caught when a manager takes the heat for the mistake of another department with no bad remarks.

Supportive: Leadership undergirds in tough times. A leader will stay an extra few minutes to make sure the next shift fully understands the job in process. That is caught when a manager cheerfully goes over to help a customer stuff envelopes when last minute changes threaten a mailing.

Customer Best: Leadership cares. Care means I want the best for the other person. A leader will make sure all the pieces of an order are packed so no damage can happen in shipping. That is caught when a manager opens the door for someone whose hands are full at the front door of the company.

Summary: Plant management is a 24/7 leadership opportunity. How you live in the hallways will flow over into your shop. Cutting corners with vendor contracts will come out in cutting corners among layout artists. No workflow quality check will replace quality leadership example.

Enjoy a Better Life Forward. ;-{) phil

> *No one like slipshod service from staff. Lead by example.*
> *Give 100% in all you do with excellence when staff is looking and when no one is looking.*

Build Better Budgets with VISION!

Budgets promote vision with numbers. They just do. A lackluster budget process represents a lackluster vision. An engaged budget process with visits to key stakeholders and excitement for new or enhanced offerings brings engagement. A comprehensive budget plan that considers and promotes the vision of your key stakeholders/customers brings good support.

Organizations work through new budgets at different times of year. However, as the New Year approaches you ponder end of year purchases, vendor deals, moratorium weeks, supply arrangements, staff, rent, and a myriad of miniscule items specific to your shop. Do it with vision.

Visibility: Get visible. Make sure the right decision makers understand you are watching out for their needs. Visit, call, listen, and integrate their ideas. Help them see how what you do accomplishes their goals. Put out a simple brag sheet on some special accomplishments.

Integrity: This is not the time to fudge numbers and hesitate. Admit defeats and mistakes. Project confidence you have plans to go forward and be there. A newer stake holder in a shop walked up to me one day, faced me squarely, and asked, "Are you going to be here for me?" Be there.

Sensitivity: Some of your best stakeholder/customers may be going through a rough budget. Learn from them. Find ways to creatively assist them through your services. Another may be planning to explode and need more. Find the balance. Make sure you are not steamrolling past another's need or vision that catches you in a surprise battle.

Influence: You are who you are. You are the expert in your services. Go ahead and be a little bold. Communicate confidence and concern and competency to your customers. Update them with new ways you can serve them and changes that might affect their future. Take care of your normal alerts concerning mundane business changes. Then consider something not as evident and show some proactive interest in their world.

Opinion: This is a good time to be assertive. Don't be aggressive. Do be assertive. If there is a conversation ongoing that might affect you and your team, put in your two cents. Show you care and show your personal ownership of serving the needs of the organization.

Necessity: Make sure all the necessities of the organization are handled in your budget. It can be easy to look to the exciting items and expansion. That is good. Daily operations must continue performed with excellence. A good service team can invisibly handle necessities and become overlooked. Communicate you are handling those pieces of necessity every month alongside all the extras and expansions.

Summary: Tying dollars in clear ways with visibility, sensitivity, influence, opinion, and necessity can give a total VISION to your budget for decision making stakeholders. They are buried in their own budgets of which you are a line item. Make it easy and supportive for them. When you need the extra push for added software, online systems improvement, facility build out, equipment, training, or people, they will remember you well.

Enjoy a Better Life Forward. ;-{) phil

Christian Power Living Tips!

Christians should be model employees and model employers. For that reason, I've included an entire section devoted to core Christian principles that should be lived in the workplace. Of course they are excellent for all, but essential for Christians.

Each starts with the admonition, Risk It! Faith requires risk. Risk is always involved in Faith. Faith is not fearsome nor ignorant. It is focused and responsible and Risky.

Risk It! Respect Authority

Take ancient authority into your workplace. Truths that transcend culture, industry, and size of business.

Psalm 19:1: The heavens declare the glory of God; and the firmament reveals openly his handywork. 2: Day unto day cries out loudly with speech, and night unto night displays and reveals knowledge. 3: There is no speech nor language, where their voice is not heard.

A winner... respects those who are superior to him and tries to learn something from them;

A Loser resents those who are superior and rationalizes their achievements.

In 1980 a young student began to lose his ability to learn. The key instructor just did not seem to be passing anything on. What was the problem? The student had left home and job to study under this learned man. Travelling 500 miles, he had risked everything, and now he seemed to be learning nothing.

Self-examination revealed a loser's attitude toward the instructor. The student had begun to rationalize, see himself better than he was. Since he wasn't singled out and acknowledged, he began internally to tear at the credibility of the instructor. The door to knowledge closed. **The gateway of learning is only opened when respect is in place**.

Being a quick learner the student adjusted. The next day he cornered the instructor and asked forgiveness. What? Ask forgiveness for a sin not committed? Yes. He asked for forgiveness from the instructor for holding anything between them. The gentle instructor forgave and forgot.

Psalm 86:5: You, Lord, are good and gracious and kind, and ready to forgive; and abundant in mercy to everyone that calls on you in their time of need.

Learning quickly returned. Now the wisdom of life flowed from instructor to student. The student went on to glean many critical lessons from this instructor which prospered him in life.

Proverbs 1:5: A wise man will hear, and will increase learning; and a man of understanding shall attain unto wise counsels:

Proverbs 1:7: The fear (respect and consideration of position and authority and person) of the LORD is the beginning (the opening of the doorway) of knowledge: but fools despise wisdom and instruction.

This principle applies not just to respecting the Lord but to respecting anyone.

Take Inventory: Do you have a lack of respect standing the way of knowledge in a relationship?

How can we be sensitive to remove the blocks to receiving knowledge and remove them quickly?

Make Application: Write what you are going to specifically do in the next 30 days about this.

Pray Respect: *Shepherd of My Soul, guide me in a manner that respects and recognizes that You have positioned others over decisions in my life for good. Even when I am confused, You are in charge.*

Risk It! Explain Not Excuse

Romans 14:11: For it is written, as I live, says the Lord, every knee shall bow to me, and every tongue shall confess to God. 12: So then every one of us shall give account of himself to God. 13: Let us not therefore judge one another anymore: but judge this rather, that no man put a stumbling block or an occasion to fall in his brother's way

A winner explains; a loser explains away

Early in life I found it profitable to have solutions. Managers, directors, executives all seemed to be unconcerned with my problems and mistakes. What they wanted was solutions. Explain the problems and offer a solution. It really did not make a difference whether I caused the problem or not. A winner goes for the solution not the excuse.

God is the same way. He really is not so much interested in punishing us. **He is interested in our growth.**

This trait of offering honest explanations with solutions is called faithfulness. When we trust a person, we are honest. When we value their opinion in the long term, we are honest. Being that way adds up to being loyal and faithful and it is so returned.

In the computer industry of big systems, there are sometimes some real messes. Blaming it on the computer never flies. It always seems profitable to simply tell people, "We are researching the problem and will get back with you." And then do it.

Doctored Madness: A certain hospital had a horrible reputation. Systems crashed daily, sometimes 3 times a day. Nurses screamed. Doctors threatened to throw equipment out the window. One doctor would come in the computer room and bang on the equipment. When the system went down, all the technicians took off their badges and hid from the hospital staff.

As a new manager, Newbie was perplexed. How do you handle this mess? First, he instructed his technicians to get their badges back on and get into the hallways. Take the heat. Own up to the problems and offer assistance. Next, he called all the head nurses and gave them an estimate of when they could expect systems so they could go back to work. Then he called the chief technicians and wanted answers. **Real answers.** When it was all over he would update the executives to the causes.

It was tough. The reputation of the department was horrid. Over time the nurses began to trust the reports. Even when it was bad news, it was trustworthy news. Systems started getting fixed and executives agreed to spend the right monies to fix the problems. Everyone turned out winners. Eventually the systems that were only up 50% of the time were up 98% of the time. Winners explain.

I Corinthians 4:1: Let a man so account of us, as of the ministers of Christ, and stewards of the mysteries of God. 2: Moreover it is required in stewards that a man be found faithful.

Watson's Venture: A story is told about Thomas Watson, then chief of IBM. Seems an executive spent a few million dollars on a project that was a total failure. He went in to Watson thinking he would be terminated. Watson looked and him and assured him that he was not about to lose the millions he had invested in the man's training.

What if he had offered excuses and blamed others? What if he had not been honest with his mistakes?

Adam had that type opportunity. He blamed Eve. What if he had just told God he miffed it and needed forgiveness?

David, king of Israel, committed murder, adultery, and things we don't even know about. But when it came time to face it, he was **honest and simply explained**. God forgave and restored him each time. David wasn't perfect, he just would not try and explain away.

Heb. 13:17: Obey them that have the rule over you, and submit yourselves: for they watch for your souls, as they that must give account, that they may do it with joy, and not with grief: for that is unprofitable for you.

This principle applies in all areas. **We all make mistakes.** We all have failures. (Failure is an event, not a person.) **We all are required to show faithfulness and loyalty by being honest and helping those around us deal with the situation**. They need the full scoop so they can work out any side issues, not so they can punish or dig it in.

Take Inventory: Do you have problem that needs fixing? Can you explain? Will you explain?

How can you get past the fear of failure through honest explanations?

Make Application: Write what you are going to specifically do in the next 30 days about this.

Pray To Be Honest In Explanation

Father, open my eyes. Let me see any hindrances to winning with Jesus. So many times in life lessons go unlearned when I don't hear Your voice. Speak clearly, Lord. Let me hear and act speedily. Open my heart, Father, to give real, honest explanations so I can stay on the road to winning.

Risk It! Find A Way

Revelation 2:7: He that hath an ear, let him hear what the Spirit says to the churches; to him that overcomes will I give to eat of the tree of life, which is in the midst of the paradise of God.

A winner says, "Let's find a way."

A Loser says, "There is no way"

Philippians 4:13: I can do all things through Christ which strengthens me.

Problems are life. A great book written some years back is entitled, "Eating Problems for Breakfast." Another great book published years ago was "Lateral Thinking". Both of these books challenge us to remember that problem solving requires getting outside our normal boxes of thought and thinking different thoughts. When we are ready to do that, **we can see incredible solutions to plaguing problems.**

Kids In Bleachers: Recently in the children's department of a large church, the problem of space for growth came up. The main area for elementary kids would only hold about 150 chairs, crammed uncomfortably with bad visibility. There had to be a way. After 15 years of looking at the problem, no one had a real viable solution. **It took getting outside the box.**

Walking through another room planned for remodel a worker struck on **an old idea with a new twist**. A choir loft seating about 75 adults was going to be torn out. Why not split the loft and reassemble it in the kids' area as bleachers? The new use of an old item would make room for 100 new kids. Not only that, but it took up little used space in the room and changed the room to a more exciting place for the kids and allowed over 250 kids to be in the room with all of them having good visibility. Add to that another idea of doubling the lumens in the lighting and the whole idea gelled. Unusable, dim space was turned into light, great space because some folks though outside the box against 15 years of "no way". (Sunbonnet: The cost was only a few dollars as the labor was volunteered along with some great carpet to cover the bleachers. The cost of purchasing bleachers and installing a new lighting system would have been over $10,000.)

1 Peter 1:7: That the trial (testing by presenting of problems)of your faith, being much more precious than of gold that perishes, though it be tried with fire, might be found unto praise and honour and glory at the appearing of Jesus Christ:

This principle applies in all areas of life. Tests, trials, opportunities, problems, glitches, frustrations, whatever you call them come up. **Persistent prayer and thought can bring new light (couldn't resist) and a different way to attack the problem. Faith pushes through to solutions.** Fear stares at the problem and gives up.

Take Inventory: Do you have a long term problem that needs fixing? How can you persist again and say, "There has to be a way!"?

What can you do today to get past the idea that you have to live with that old problem?

Make Application: Write what you are going to specifically do in the next 30 days about this.

Pray To Be A Problem Solver: *Father, quicken my mind and heart. Encourage faith in me to believe again for something on which I have given up hope. You are so real and alive and active in everything that is. Stretch my faith. Let me be like the one who said to Jesus, "Lord, I believe. Help my unbelief." Give me the courage to try a new approach and see Your hand displayed.*

Risk It! Go On Through.

To go through a problem is to conquer it and create new paths. Go through. Don't go around it.

Psalm 95:8: Harden not your heart, as in the provocation, and as in the day of temptation in the wilderness

A winner goes through a problem.

A loser tries to go around a problem.

Philippians 4:13: I can do all things through Christ which strengthens me.

Problems are life. Sound like the last chapter? You are right. It is not the same though. What makes a winner a conqueror, an overcomer, is the problems they face and conquer. You will have problems. *1Peter 4:12:" Beloved, think it not strange concerning the fiery trial which is to try you, as though some strange thing happened unto you:"*

The question is will you go through or around?

Going around. The children of Israel spent 40 years going around their problems. When they were offered the land of opportunity, they chose to stay away and not deal with their problems. What was their problem? Discord, lack of submission to leadership, unbelief, selfishness… basically just a lot of reliance on themselves and little on God.

Going through. After that 40 year phase, a new set of children rose up and went through their problems. They stuck together, defended each other, and took the blessings by going through their problems.

Going around. The United States is full of men and women going around their problems. Insecurity, lack of knowledge on how to be a dad/mom/husband/wife, lack of commitment, irresponsibility, and self-fulfillment keeps them from sticking with their families and spouses and friends. It's easier to go around.

Going through. My heroes are the ones who overcome their insecurities, lack of knowledge, lack of commitment, irresponsibility, and self-fulfillment, replace it with security in Jesus, knowledge from the Word, commitment to what counts, responsibility even when it hurts, and other fulfillment, and stick with the program. It is not easy. It is incredibly rewarding.

Hebrews 4:14: Seeing then that we have a great high priest, that is passed into the heavens, Jesus the Son of God, let us hold fast our profession. 15: For we have not an high priest which cannot be touched with the feeling of our infirmities; but was in all points tempted like as we are, yet without sin. 16: Let us therefore come boldly unto the throne of grace, that we may obtain mercy, and find grace to help in time of need.

Principle is principle is principle. Relationships, work issues, projects, and hobbies all present problems. When you allow others to help in the process, you prosper quicker. Sometimes they have the solution you need. Always, Jesus has the solution you need.

Take Inventory: Where do you have a problem that you have circumvented but not solved?

Are you ready to do what it takes to solve it?

Have you ever felt like getting mad at God because of a problem? Did you go around the problem or through it?

Overcoming. As I write this I am praying for five relationships where someone has come to me in the last week and asked for prayer. They are GOING THROUGH! Anger, alcohol, and accusations make for hard lives. You can GO THROUGH. You can overcome. It takes both involved in the relationship, but it can be done. Who are you praying for?

Make Application

Write what you are going to specifically do in the next 30 days about this.

Pray for Push through Power: *Father of Strength and Conquest, Your word tells me those that follow You and Your way will do great exploits. We are not a common race. We are uncommonly filled with all things necessary for life and for Godliness. Make me like You. Make me to be creative and persistent in all things to see solutions and fresh progress.*

Risk It! The Better Way Mentality

Every progressive effort starts with a step toward change and a holy dissatisfaction with status quo.

Philipians3:13: Brethren, I count not myself to have apprehended: but this one thing I do, forgetting those things which are behind, and reaching forth unto those things which are before,

A winner …says, "There is a better way."

A loser…. says, "That is the way it has always been done around here."

Philippians 4:13: I can do all things through Christ which strengthens me.

Life is full of opportunities to continue to do the same things. One man defined insanity this way: Doing the same thing over and over and expecting different results. Expectations, persistence of others, voices from the past, and other forces impugn on our ability to think new, creative thoughts about what we do.

How do you get into the "better way" mentality? A favorite saying of mine is, **"If it ain't broke, break it."** What? Don't you mean, "If it ain't broke, don't fix it." No, I meant what I wrote. "If it ain't broke, break it." Many times we build traditional barriers around an activity structured on preference and our limited understanding at the time. A man displayed curiosity about the way his wife cooked a roast beef. She would always cut the ends off. Thinking there must be a great culinary secret to this method he asked her why. "I don't know," she replied, "my mother taught me that way."

Pressed for information on the private process he went to her mother. "I don't know," she replied, "my mother taught me that way." Perplexed he drove to the matron of the family's home and asked again. "Oh," she quickly responded, "my roasting pan was too short to hold the full roast."

Most processes need to be repaired regularly. Now, you don't want to tear up a good thing, so there are many other rules of change and improvement like: Always give a change time to go through the curve of lagging productivity until people learn the new way and become adept before implementing the next change. AND any change will be resisted in strength in direct proportion to its' potential for improvement.

Life is full of processes and a "better way" mentality will protect you from foolish failure. A computer tech went out to resolve a problem one day in an executive secretary's office. Seemed that every time she printed a letter she first had to print all the letters she had ever printed. It took an half a box of paper to print a letter! The cost and time of doing her job that way finally overcame her embarrassment and she asked for help. The fix was simple. She was simply doing what she had been shown. Open a file, go to the end, type the letter, and print it. The problem was she had only be given one file name and all the letters since she began her job were in one file that she printed each time according to explicit instructions. Absurd? Real. Fortune 500 company. Executive secretary doing something that needed to be broken.

What about the way we converse with others? What about how we walk into a meeting? What about how we greet our friends? Are those processes that could use some "better way" mentality?

Jesus broke the mold for some in the way they treated their parents in a story related in Matthew 15. God gave a principle. Honor your fathers and mothers. They made a rule that kept them out conveniently. Tradition overruled wisdom and principle, and Jesus saw through the smoke. *Matt 15:6: Thus have ye made the commandment of God of none effect by your tradition.*

Therefore, since we are surrounded by such a great cloud of witnesses, let us throw off everything that hinders and the sin that so easily entangles, and let us run with perseverance the race marked out for us. Let us fix our eyes on Jesus, the author and perfecter of our faith, who for the joy set before him endured the cross, scorning its shame, and sat down at the right hand of the throne of God. Hebrews 12: 1-2 NIV.

Principle is principle is principle. Relationships, work issues, projects, and hobbies all present problems. When you allow others to help in the process, you prosper quicker. Sometimes they have the solution you need. **Always, Jesus has the solution you need.**

Take Inventory: Where do you have a process, a way of doing things that really could use some improvement by being broken?

Are you ready to give up personal preferences and do what it takes to "break it and make it better"?

Can you think of a scripture to apply that can help you into "better way" mentality?

Make Application: Write what you are going to specifically do in the next 30 days about this.

Pray To Be Changeable: *Father, quicken my mind and heart. Life is full of processes. You know the one that needs breaking and bettering at this moment. God, I can get so confused with all of the items in life. What item can I work on today? What am I doing that really does more damage than good? Where can I get a lift seeing you touch a new area of my life and give me a creative fresh approach? Cleanse my thinking, Lord. Jesus, be my wisdom, be my source, be my life giver. Holy Spirit release the fresh wind of Your brooding. Brood over my thoughts and bring order to their chaos that I might see clearly what You want to create.*

Risk It! Change

Every great innovation began with a resistance to status quo. The greatest status quo that hinders is personal character.

Phil:4:8: Finally, brethren, whatsoever things are true, whatsoever things are honest, whatsoever things are just, whatsoever things are pure, whatsoever things are lovely, whatsoever things are of good report; if there be any virtue, and if there be any praise, think on these things. 9: Those things, which ye have both learned, and received, and heard, and seen in me, do: and the God of peace shall be with you.

A winner …shows he is sorry by acting differently.

A loser…. says, "I'm sorry", but continues to do it again.

Philippians 4:13: I can do all things through Christ who strengthens me.

You would like to get victory over weaknesses, wouldn't you? That is what Jesus is all about. In the book of the Revelation there are many promises to the one who overcomes, stays until the end, "takes a lickin' and keeps on tickin", keeps moving on. Our weaknesses, insecurities, nuances of personality haunt us in the path of the winner. Over and over we will make mistakes, glitch in performance, slip climbing the ladder, fall on our face, and get egg on our face, boondoggle……sin.

Yes, **one key word used for sin in the Bible is simply to miss the mark.** Shoot at a goal and miss it. Decide we want to be loving and react with anger. Decide to keep our minds pure then fill it with trashy books, magazines, and the boob tube. Promise to a wife or son or daughter or friend or neighbor or coworker or employee or employer and then not follow through. Sin.

The question is, "What do we do then?" Do we take a winner's stance or a loser's escape? Do we face up, fess up, and clean the mess up? Or do we put on a face, say, "I'm sorry", and fade away only to do it again and again?

Winners change. **Winners find a way to do life differently the next time.**

Some years back a famous jewel thief was being interviewed over his life. He had spent many years in prison. His modus operandi was to only steal from the rich and famous. The interviewer asked him what his biggest theft was. His reply was, "Me." The explanation was simple. He had stolen his own life. What could have been a great creative mind used productively was used to steal and hurt.   When you refuse to change and use the talents and strengths God gives you, you are stealing from yourself. Your time, energy, and talent go into actions that only produce hurt and pain for you and others. Why not change to a better way? Why not get a new thought process and quit doing what doesn't work, what only hurts?

Therefore, since we are surrounded by such a great cloud of witnesses, let us throw off everything that hinders and the sin that so easily entangles, and let us run with perseverance the race marked out for us. Let us fix our eyes on Jesus, the author and perfecter of our faith, who for the joy set before him endured the cross, scorning its shame, and sat down at the right hand of the throne of God.   Hebrews 12: 1-2 NIV.

Take Inventory: What needs changing in your thought life?

What can you fill your mind with that will cause the old thoughts to go out and new ones come in?

Make a date with destiny. When are you going to start?

Make Application: Write what you are going to specifically do in the next 30 days about this.

Let's Pray: *Father, it is tough to give up my habits and hang-ups. I like them. They like me. They fit my life. Everyone who knows me, knows me as I am. And You want me to change. I need strength. Empower me with Your Holy Spirit*

Risk It! Stand Ground. Give Ground.

Pick your battles. There is a time to stand and a time to give ground. Use wisdom. Move purposefully.

Philippians 1:27: But whatever happens, make sure that your everyday life is worthy of the gospel of Christ. So that whether I do come and see you, or merely hear about you from a distance, I may know that you are standing fast in a united spirit, battling with a single mind for the faith of the gospel and not caring two straws for your enemies. (J.B. Phillips translation).

A winner….. Knows when to fight and when to compromise.

A loser ….. Fights over the wrong things and compromises at the wrong time.

Hebrews 12:14 Let it be your ambition to live at peace with all men and to achieve holiness "without which no man shall see the Lord" (J.B. Phillips translation)

Winners know when to fight to win and when to give. In the song, "The Gambler", the advice was given, "You got to know when to hold 'em, know when to fold 'em, know when to walk away, and know when to run." There is a fight worth fighting, and there are items in life not worth the effort.

Winston Churchill in the darkest hours of England's battles with Germany had this sense. When others wanted to lay down and give up he stood ground and challenged, "Never give up. Never give up. Never give up." The war was won over courage and tenacity and knowing the fight needed to be fought.

You have to know when to fight. After living in their new home for a year, the Newbies had a major problem. Sewage came running over into the downstairs bath, living room, and entry foyer. What a mess! Massive cleanup, roto-rooter, and a few days of showering at the neighbors did not fix it. The city claimed the problem was theirs, the plumber claimed the city needed to fix it. Two great neighbors and a day of digging exposed a major city problem. Out they came, and yes, they fixed it. They dug 14 feet deep, repaired the sewer main, and replaced fences they had to tear down. But, they didn't take care of the carpet and house. Forms, forms, and more forms, telephone calls, working with city attorneys, and a lot of prayer resulted in a surprise. One night the local city councilman called to alert the Newbies that their reimbursement request was scheduled to get the hatchet the next day at the city council meeting. Newbie showed up at the council meeting of this large metropolitan community. Deep in the docket was a line item scratching the claim along with over 30 other homeowners. What could he do? Fight. Fight for his wife to get carpet. Fight for restoration. Fight he did. First in prayer, then in rhetoric. "Mayor, my friends and I dug a 7 foot deep hole to show the city that the problem was theirs, I am willing to dig a 7 foot deep rhetorical hole to help the council see it needs to pay these costs." The council halted him right there and offered to pay a reasonable settlement. No one else was awarded that day. The clerk could not believe it when she issued the check.

You have to know when to give and compromise. The budget battle was intense. Hundreds of thousands of dollars in expansion monies were battled over by several departments. Systems executives along with Newbie decided to withdraw and let the money go to retail remodels. Eight months later accounting in an executive meeting moved $50,000.00 to systems and challenged them, "See what you can do with that." After 30 days of scramble and results, they gave them another $400,000.00 to spend moved from retail remodels.

Take Inventory: Where do you need to fight? Does someone need defending?

Where do you need to lay down your arms? Is it better to give now and win a friend?

Make Application: Write what you are going to specifically do in the next 30 days about this.

Let's Pray: *Okay, God of Glory, Lord of Hosts (Armies Camped for War), I need Your wisdom. There is a time to stand and a time to sit. There is a time to run forward and a time to hold present ground. Show me the most effective use of my time right now. Give me courage to engage the enemy for good in all areas of my life.*

Risk It!

Winners take risks. They are unafraid of loss. The balance of gains over losses motivates.

Psalm 20:6: Now I know that the LORD saves (brings out of trouble, restores, and strengthens) His anointed; He will hear him (and respond to his rallying call for help) from His holy heaven with the saving strength of His right hand (the hand of power and ability, the hand at which Jesus represents His). 7: Some trust in chariots, and some in horses (some trust in their riches and alliances and abilities and mental acuity): but we will remember the name of the LORD our God. 8: They (our enemies and all those who trust in their own strength) are brought down and fallen: but we are risen, and stand upright.

Winners are not afraid of losing or making mistakes.

They are willing to take risks necessary to succeed in life.

Life means risk. Life means taking chances that cause loss. Loss of friends, loss of co-workers, loss of status, loss of power, loss of control, loss of understanding of those important to you, loss of money.. All these are losses a winner decides at times must be risked. "No pain, no gain. Know gain, know pain." some would say. Life means risk. Risk means loss. Risk also means winning.

Edison risked until he found the right element for light bulbs. Once on a comment that it took fifty thousand tries before he got results, he explained, "Results? Why I have gotten a lot of results. I know fifty thousand things that won't work."

Ray Kroc became an outstanding business leader. Yet, for years he failed at every business attempt. It was so bad his wife was ready to leave him on his last venture. Seems he sold out everything to buy a few hamburger joints owned by some brothers named McDonald. You guessed it. That was the start of the McDonald's chain of restaurants that made the Krocs multi-millionaires. Winners keep trying. (By the way, his wife stuck it out.)

Those secure in Jesus are unafraid of risk because they know He will back them up. They know they can make a mistake and be put back on track.

Psalm 37:23: The steps of a good man are ordered by the LORD: and he delights in his way. 24: Though he fall, he shall not be utterly cast down: for the LORD upholds him with his hand. 25: I have been young, and now am old; yet have I not seen the righteous forsaken, nor his seed begging bread. 26: He is ever merciful, and lends; and his seed is blessed.

Take Inventory: Pensive?

Trying to make a decision?

What is it?

Write it down. Write down the good and bad about it. Pray about it. Listen to God. Commit it to Him. Decide. Don't let fear hold you down.

Make Application: Write what you are going to specifically do in the next 30 days about this.

Pray To Be Bold: *Father, encourage me. Strengthen me to take that step of faith in Your leading. I am weak, Father. I fail. I am made of grass and wither in the noon sun, but You cause a shadow to cover me. Let the cool breathe of Your Spirit blow over me and freshen my day. Though I fall, I will get up and go again. You will cause me to succeed.*

Risk It! Be an Able Also.

The intensity of being a contributor versus a consumer brings us to moments of challenged ability. Be one that is **able in the moment needed** and others will entrust greatness into your hands.

2Tm:2:2: And the things that thou hast heard of me among many witnesses, the same commit thou to faithful men, who shall be able to teach others also.

Winners Make Commitments.

Losers Make Promises.

In these few short words to Timothy, Paul revealed a tremendous portion of the key to his winning life. Look at the word choices. Among Many Witnesses. The Same. Commit. Faithful Men. Able Also.

Among many witnesses. **Paul was not afraid for his life to be tested against witnesses**. His words were true and he stayed with them. What witnesses heard years before still was true of his life. Timothy was charged to make sure solid teaching, life, and words passed on to other men of commitment.

The same. **Paul was open in his life**. He committed himself to being like Jesus. The same yesterday, today, and forever.

Commit. Paul was committal. **He made commitments and expected others to do the same.**

Faithful men.   These are hard to find. **Paul never gave up**. Betrayed continually, he never gave up looking for faithful men.

Able also. We can be an "able also". **An "able also" does the same in making commitment, sticking with it, being faithful, following through, endures all things, bears all things, believes all things, hopes all things.**

Promises are cheap. "I'll be there." MEANS "If it fits the pressures of the moment's right before." OR "Whatever it takes to get you to quit asking." "Til death do us part." MEANS "Until I redefine what I meant." OR "Until I don't want to handle the pressures anymore face to face."

Commitment is expensive. "I'll be there." MEANS "Whatever the cost, I'll rearrange life to get me there." "Til death do us part." MEANS "I will stick it out though I may not feel like it. "I will take control of my feelings and bring them to submission in Christ."

*Psalm 15:1: LORD, who shall abide in thy tabernacle? Who shall dwell in thy holy hill? 2: He that **walks uprightly**, and works righteousness, and **speaks the truth in his heart.** 3: He that backbites not with his tongue, nor does evil to his neighbor, nor takes up a reproach against his neighbor. 4: In whose eyes a vile person is contemned; but he honors them that fear the LORD. **He that swears to his own hurt, and changes not.** 5: He that puts not out his money to usury, nor taketh reward against the innocent. He that doeth these things shall never be moved.*

Take Inventory: What does it mean to be an "ABLE ALSO"?

What changes do I have to make?

Are there repairs that need to be done to broken commitments?

When am I willing to start?

Make Application: Write what you are going to specifically do in the next 30 days about this.

Pray To Be an Able Also

Father, make me an "ABLE ALSO". Change the way I promise to commitment. Instill in me faithfulness. When I am faithless, You are faith-full. Make me like Jesus, the same yesterday, today, and forever. Psalm 51:10: Create in me a clean heart, O God; and renew a right spirit within me. 11: Cast me not away from thy presence; and take not thy holy spirit from me. 12: Restore unto me the joy of thy salvation; and uphold me with thy free spirit. 13: Then will I teach transgressors thy ways; and sinners shall be converted unto thee.

Prologue

That should be enough for this edition of Manage Well. You'll notice there are more than 31 entries. Okay, well there are four from the flip book that are not in here and a few from other notes that are in this group. We'll save those for the next book alongside more tips on developing high performance teams, developing yourself, and exceeding expectations. And, of course, you have the bonus section for the Christian power living tips.

Join me on LinkedIn (phillarsonokc)

Find me on Facebook. (communitytransformationinitiative)

Read online shepherdok.com

We Own the Future! Tenemos El Futuro.

Made in the USA
San Bernardino, CA
19 September 2015